GEORGE WHITEFIELD

GEORGE WHITEFIELD

BY

MICHAEL A. G. HAYKIN

EP BOOKS
Faverdale North
Darlington
DL3 0PH, England

www.epbooks.org
sales@epbooks.org

EP BOOKS are distributed in the USA by:
JPL Fulfillment
3741 Linden Avenue Southeast,
Grand Rapids, MI 49548.

E-mail: sales@jplfulfillment.com
Tel: 877.683.6935

First EP Books edition published 2014

ISBN: 978–1–78397–065–0

British Library Cataloguing in Publication Data available

To Gregory A. Wills,
for his friendship in the very same gospel
that Whitefield loved and preached.

TABLE OF CONTENTS

Timeline

1714 Dec. 16   Born in the Bell Inn, Gloucester

1732   Matriculated at Pembroke College, Oxford

1735, Spring   Converted

1736, June 20   Ordained deacon at Gloucester

June 27   Preached first sermon, St. Mary de Crypt, Gloucester

1738, Feb.–May   First voyage to America

May–Sept.   Ministry in the southern colonies

Sept.–Dec.   Voyage home to England

1739, January 14 Ordained priest in Church of England

1739, February 17 Began open-air preaching

9

Summer	Published *The Indwelling of the Spirit, the Common Privilege of All Believers*
August–Oct.	Second voyage to America
Dec. 16	Preached *What think ye of Christ?* at Williamsburg, Virginia
1740, Sept. 24	Visited Harvard
Oct. 17– 22	Visited Jonathan Edwards at Northampton, Massachusetts
1740–1742	Conflict with the Wesley brothers over the doctrines of Calvinism and the doctrine of Christian perfection
1741, Jan.–March	Voyage back to England
	Christ, the Believer's Wisdom, Righteousness, Sanctification and Redemption published
July 24	First visit to Scotland
Nov. 14	Married Elizabeth James of Abergavenny, Wales
1742, July	Present at the revival at Cambuslang, Scotland

1743, Oct. 4	His son, John Whitefield, born
1744, Feb. 8	Buried his infant son
June 26	Attacked and almost murdered in Plymouth
Aug.–Oct.	Third voyage to America
1744–1748	Ministry in America
1748, March	Left America for Bermuda
March 15	Reached Bermuda and begins a stay of about two months
June–July	Voyage from Bermuda to England
Sept. 14	Arrived in Edinburgh for third visit to Scotland
1751, May	Second visit to Ireland
July	Fifth visit to Scotland
Aug.–Nov.	Fourth voyage to America
1752, April-May	Return voyage to England
1754–1755	Fifth preaching tour in America

1757, June-July	Third visit to Ireland & physically attacked in Dublin (early July)
1763–1765	Sixth trip to America
1768, June 15	Final visit to Scotland; preached in Edinburgh
Aug. 9	Death of Elizabeth Whitefield, his wife
1769, Sept.	Left England for final voyage to America
1769–1770	Final ministry in America
1770, Sept. 30	Died at Newburyport, Massachusetts
1771, Oct. 11	Phillis Wheatley's *An Elegiac Poem, On ... George Whitefield* published

1

Remembering George Whitefield

In 1835 Francis Alexander Cox and James Hoby, two prominent English Baptists who were visiting fellow Baptists in the United States, made a side trip to Newburyport, Massachusetts, to view the tomb of George Whitefield. The 'grand itinerant' had died on September 30, 1770, at the home of Jonathan Parsons, pastor of the town's First Presbyterian Church, known also as Old South. He had been interred two days later in a vault below what is now the centre aisle of this church, where, along with the coffins of Parsons and another pastor of the church, Joseph Prince, his remains were on display throughout the nineteenth century. In fact, it was not until 1932 that the coffin in which Whitefield's remains lay was covered over with a slate slab.

Cox and Hoby later recalled descending with some difficulty into the subterraneous vault where Whitefield was buried. As they did so, they remembered that 'deep expectant emotions thrilled our bosoms'. They sat on the two other coffins in the vault and watched as the upper half of the lid of Whitefield's coffin was opened on its hinges 'to reveal the skeleton secrets of the narrow prison-house'. They 'contemplated and handled the skull', while they 'thought of his devoted life, his blessed death, his high and happy destiny' and 'whispered [their] adorations of the grace that formed him both for earth and heaven'. What makes this scene even more *outré* is that the skeletal remains that Cox and Hoby viewed were not intact. The main bone of Whitefield's right arm had been stolen some years earlier by another Englishman. It was not until either the late 1830s or even the 1840s that the thief's conscience brought him to the point of sending the bone back across the Atlantic in a small wooden box!

This account is a powerful reminder of the fact that of all the great preachers raised up in the transatlantic Evangelical Revival in the eighteenth century none gripped the public mind and imagination more than George Whitefield. During his lifetime, the Congregationalist Joseph Williams, a merchant from Kidderminster with a keen interest in spiritual renewal, rightly termed him the 'Father' of those seeking to advance the revival. Henry St. John, Viscount Bolingbroke, who 'professed himself a deist', was forced to exclaim, after hearing Whitefield preach: 'the most extraordinary man of our times, the most commanding eloquence, unquenchable zeal, unquestionable piety'. On the other side of the Atlantic, Benjamin Colman and William Cooper, both New England pastors, viewed Whitefield as 'the wonder of the age' and were convinced that 'no man more employs the pens, and fills up the conversation of people, than he does at this day'. Shortly after the evangelist's death Augustus Montague Toplady, author of the famous hymn 'Rock of Ages, cleft for me', remembered him as 'the apostle of the English empire'. And looking back from the following century, John Foster, the Baptist essayist, was sure that with 'the doubtful exception of Wickliffe, no man probably ever excited in this island [i.e. the British Isles] so profound, and extended, and prolonged a sensation in the public mind, by personal addresses to the understanding and conscience, on the subject of religion'.

By the twentieth century, however, Whitefield's name had been eclipsed by his fellow Evangelical, John Wesley, who had come to epitomize the eighteenth-century Evangelical Revival and who left a world-wide denominational body, the Methodists, to remember him. Rediscovery of Whitefield's central importance to the Church of the eighteenth century did not really take place until the 1970s when the Canadian pastor-historian Arnold Dallimore, who had been studying Whitefield's life and thought since the early 1950s, had his massive two-volume biography of Whitefield published by the Banner of Truth. Under God, Dallimore's life of Whitefield has had an enormous impact on the global Church. One constantly comes across men and women from North America, Britain, Australia, and South Africa, not to mention other places, whose lives have been radically changed through the reading of these volumes. As Sinclair Ferguson has rightly noted: Dallimore's 'wonderful study of Whitefield is one of the great biographies of the Christian Church'. In fact, it was the gift of this two-volume set at the time of my doctoral graduation in 1982 that set me on the road to embracing the theology that stirred the heart and mind of Whitefield.

Given that there are now a number of good studies of Whitefield's life, I have especially sought to capture key facets of his thought in the brief compass of this book. As Baptist historian Owen Strachan has rightly noted, if we are to 'regain the essence of George Whitefield, then ... [we] must return to the very core of this man's identity: the beliefs he held and the message he preached'. So, after outlining the era in which Whitefield lived and ministered in chapter 2 and giving an overview of Whitefield's life and ministry in chapter 3, the next five chapters look at five key areas of his ministry: his passion for preaching the gospel, his emphasis on the new birth and justification by faith alone, his defence of a biblical understanding of holiness especially in contrast to John Wesley's view of Christian perfection, his commitment to Calvinism and its distinctive spirituality, and finally the example of his impact upon one denominational grouping, the Baptists. Since the 1980s I have spent much time and energy tracing the pathway of revival among the English Baptists, my theological and spiritual forebears, and this small study of Whitefield provided the ideal opportunity to look at the immense contribution Whitefield made to this awakening. Whitefield never lost his love for the Anglican Church in which he was reared, but God used him to richly bless others beyond the borders of his own denomination. And for that, I am immensely thankful.

ACKNOWLEDGEMENTS

Biographies may be written by single authors, but nearly always they involve the help of others. This one is no exception. I am particularly indebted to Dr Ian Hugh Clary, my research assistant, especially with regard to his knowledge of Arnold Dallimore's biography of Whitefield; and to Matthew Haste, one of my Ph.D. students at The Southern Baptist Theological Seminary, for the use of two sections of a paper he did on Whitefield for one of my doctoral seminars. Matthew gave me permission to edit and rework those sections, and so use them in the chapter on Whitefield's Calvinistic piety. I am also thankful to Joshua Press for permission to use large sections of my introduction to *The revived Puritan: The spirituality of George Whitefield* (Dundas, ON: Joshua Press, 2000). About five paragraphs about Whitefield and the American Baptists in Chapter 8 are taken from a forthcoming book— Anthony L. Chute, Nathan A. Finn, and Michael A. G. Haykin, *The Baptist Story: From English Sect to Global Movement* (Nashville, TN: B&H, 2015)—and are used with permission. Dr Joe Harrod and Dustin Bruce, both Fellows of the Andrew Fuller Center for Baptist Studies at The Southern Baptist Theological Seminary, were also a great help, as was Janice van Eck.

I have dedicated this small study of Whitefield's life and thought to Dr Gregory A. Wills, Academic Dean of the School of Theology at The Southern Baptist Theological Seminary, for his friendship and his unflagging encouragement of my work as a scholar.

2

LIVING IN THE
EIGHTEENTH CENTURY

The era in which Whitefield began his remarkable ministry was anything but hospitable to biblical Christianity. Summing up the characteristics of transatlantic British society in the opening decades of the eighteenth century, Oxford historian John Walsh, for instance, lists the following: a noticeable decay of ministerial authority, the growth of rationalism and a massive intellectual assault on supernatural Christianity, the spread of material wealth and 'luxury', the frivolity of the young and an indifference on their part to spiritual matters, and a sense of spiritual powerlessness among Christians.

Attestation of this description is found in both public documents and private testimonies. Here is the witness of one author, the London Baptist theologian Benjamin Keach, writing in 1701:

> *Was ever sodomy so common in a Christian nation, or so notoriously and frequently committed, as by too palpable evidences it appears to be, in and about this city, notwithstanding the clear light of the gospel which shines therein, and the great pains taken to reform the abominable profaneness that abounds? Is it not a wonder the patience of God hath not consumed us in his wrath, before this time? Was ever swearing, blasphemy, whoring, drunkenness, gluttony, self-love, and covetousness, at such a height, as at this time here?*

Despite the presence of a number of gospel-centred ministries like that of Keach and various societies which had been created to bring about moral reform, homosexuality, profanity, sexual immorality, drunkenness and gluttony were widespread. And the next three decades saw little improvement.

The moral tone of the nation was set in many ways by its monarchs and leading politicians. George I was primarily interested in food, horses, and women. He divorced his wife when he was thirty-four and thereafter consorted with a series of mistresses. Sir Robert Walpole, prime minister from 1722 to 1742, lived in undisguised adultery with his mistress, Maria Skerrett, whom he married after his wife died. As the English historian J. H. Plumb has noted of aristocratic circles in the early eighteenth century, the women 'hardly bothered with the pretence of virtue, and the possession of lovers and mistresses was regarded as a commonplace, a matter for gossip but not reproach'. Not surprisingly other segments of society simply followed suit. Pornographic literature, for instance, multiplied almost unchecked. Newspapers advertised such things as the services of gigolos and cures for venereal disease, and one could purchase guide-books to the numerous brothels in London. It was, in the words of writer and journalist Selina Hastings—a descendant of her eighteenth-century namesake, the Countess of Huntingdon—'an age when atheism was fashionable, sexual morals lax, and drinking and gambling at a pitch of profligacy that he never since been equalled'.

Social conditions were equally bleak. While many of the rich indulged themselves and all of their whims, the lot of the ordinary man and woman was quite different. For a variety of economic causes, the towns of England in the eighteenth century were the pioneers of the Industrial Revolution and as a result they mushroomed. The population of London, the capital, more than doubled to over a million and was the largest city in the western world. At the beginning of the eighteenth century, England's populace was small and the country had a predominantly rural and village character. In 1701 there were 5.1 million people; but by 1751 there were 5.8 million, a number that had risen to 8.7 million by 1801. In 1750 about 15% of this population lived in towns; by 1800, 25% of the population lived in an urban environment. Many men and women came to these cities from rural poverty, hoping to find a decent living. But adequate housing could not keep up with the demand, and those who most needed the shelter lacked sufficient funds to purchase it. Consequently, houses were desperately overcrowded. In a large industrial centre like Manchester, for example, ten people living in a room was common. Such rooms were often without furniture and lacked even beds. The occupants would sleep close together on wood shavings for warmth. Disease was rampant and unchecked: smallpox, typhus, typhoid, and dysentery made death a very familiar figure. The social conditions of England in the early eighteenth century are comparable to underdeveloped countries today. Life-expectancy was about 35 years of age, with high infant mortality.

From such a dismal situation many sought escape in drink. Beer had always been a central part of English life. But in the eighteenth century many turned to something far more potent: gin. By mid-century, the consumption of poorly distilled, and often virtually poisonous, gin was eleven million gallons a year. Some idea of the debilitation wrought by this plague may be grasped in terms of a simple item of record. In one area of London, for instance, comprising two thousand houses or so, 506 were gin shops. One contemporary novelist, Henry Fielding, estimated that in London one hundred thousand people drank gin as their principal means of sustenance. The sort of suffering that such consumption of gin brought in its wake is well illustrated by a news item from 1748 which reads as follows: 'At a christening at Beddington in Surrey the nurse was so intoxicated that after she had undressed the child, instead of laying it in the cradle she put it behind a large fire, which burnt it to death in a few minutes'!

But what of the Church—could it not make a difference? The dominant religious grouping was the Church of England, which was the established church of the land. But it was largely helpless when it came to dealing with social and moral problems. First of all, the Church of England was primarily a rural-based denomination. Despite the large-scale population shift towards industrial, urban centres, the Church of England stayed in the country. Then, the bishops in the eighteenth-century Church of England were by and large, in the words of Plumb, 'first and foremost politicians', not men of the Spirit. 'There is a worldliness', Plumb continues, 'about eighteenth-century [bishops] which no amount of apologetics can conceal'. They undertook their clerical duties 'only as political duties allowed'. The worldliness of these bishops showed in other ways as well. Jonathan Trelawny, Bishop of Winchester, used to 'excuse himself for his much swearing by saying he swore as a baronet, and not as a bishop'! Such bishops had neither the time nor the interest to promote church renewal. Of course, the decadence of church leadership was by no means absolute; but the net effect of worldly bishops was to squash effective reform.

Moreover, the attention of far too many of the clergy under these bishops was taken up with such avocations as philosophy, biology, agriculture, chemistry, literature, law, politics, fox-hunting, drinking—anything but pastoral ministry and the spiritual nurture of the people in the parish. There were, of course, a goodly number of Church of England ministers who did not have the resources to indulge themselves in such pursuits, since they barely eked out a living. But few of them—wealthy or poor—preached anything but dry, unaffecting moralistic sermons. The mindset of the first half of the eighteenth century gloried in reason, moderation and decorum. The preaching of the day dwelt largely upon themes of morality and decency and lacked 'any element of holy excitement, of passionate pleading, of heroic challenge, of winged imagination'. In a diary kept by a shopkeeper named Thomas Turner from East Hoathly, Sussex, such preaching was insightfully criticized as an:

> *idle lazy way of preaching, which many of our clergy are got into, seeming rather to make self-interest the motive for the exercising their profession than the eternal happiness and salvation of men's souls. To which if we add the intolerable degree of pride and covetousness predominant in too many of our clergy, we need not wonder at our degeneracy from the strict piety with which our forefathers worshipped God in the first ages of Christianity.*

THE EXAMPLE OF WILLIAM GRIMSHAW

William Grimshaw of Haworth, who was converted in 1741, powerfully illustrates the sort of Anglican clergyman Thomas Turner had in mind in the quote above. Grimshaw was born in September of 1708 at Brindle, Lancashire, not far from Preston. There is very little reliable data about his early years, though there is some evidence that his parents, nominal Christians at the time, raised him with a sense of moral responsibility to a holy God. At the age of seventeen, Grimshaw went up to Cambridge, where he was admitted in April, 1726 to Christ's College as a sizar (poor student)—Whitefield would be in a similar position at Oxford University.

It is important to realize that academic standards at Cambridge during the eighteenth century were not that high. The majority of the professors did not lecture or tutor the students, but spent their time writing and left the direction of the students' academic studies to tutors or tutorial assistants. Academic requirements for completing a degree course were minimal. Moreover, as John Wesley noted about the moral state of Cambridge University and its counterpart in Oxford: 'the moment a young man sets foot in either Oxford or Cambridge he is surrounded by company of all kinds ... with loungers and triflers of every sort; with men who no more concern themselves with learning than religion'.

During his first couple of years at Cambridge, Grimshaw, however, applied himself to his studies and later described himself at this time as 'sober and diligent'. But this soon changed as Grimshaw gave way to the moral turpitude of university life. In his own words, he fell in 'with bad company' and 'learned to drink, swear, and what not'. Given his style of living, it is amazing that throughout the latter period of time he hoped to become a clergyman upon graduation. As he put it, he aimed at such because it would give him a steady source of income, a roof over his head and bread upon his plate. What theology he had was now of the Deistic variety, in which the robust Christianity of the Reformers and Puritans was subjected to the scrutiny of human reason and all that seemingly could not pass the test of rationality was rejected or played down. Thus the very concept of revelation was discarded along with the doctrine of the Trinity and the deity of Christ.

Despite his evident lack of qualifications to be a minister in the Church of England, Grimshaw was ordained as a deacon in April of 1731 and a year later as a priest. The men and women in his parish of Todmorden, west Yorkshire, were described by one contemporary as 'wild, uncouth, rugged as their native hills'. But it was here at Todmorden that Grimshaw began to be awakened to the fact that he was in a desperate spiritual state.

The godlessness of Grimshaw's life was all too typical of eighteenth-century clerics. Like many other ministers throughout the length and breadth of England, Grimshaw spent his time fishing and hunting, drinking and playing cards. Instead of being times of spiritual nurture, his pastoral visits were occasions for heavy drinking. And like other ministers of this ilk, he thought nothing of the vows he had made when ordained to preach the gospel and to be the spiritual guide of those in the parish. John Newton, who wrote an early biography of Grimshaw, noted that he did 'his duty, as the phrase is, in the church, once on the Lord's day ... With this his conscience was satisfied. Whether his flock was satisfied, he neither knew nor cared'.

The immediate cause of Grimshaw's awakening was the death of a five-week-old girl, the first child of a young couple in the parish, James and Susan Scholfield. The mother awoke one awful morning to find the child she dearly loved stone dead. For a period of time Susan's mind became unhinged and she continued to tend to the child as if it were alive. Grimshaw was called for, but could only advise the parents 'to put away all gloomy thoughts, and to get into merry company, and divert themselves, and all would soon be right'. Not surprisingly, this advice proved utterly ineffective to help the parents overcome their grief. Grimshaw was again sent for and this time admitted he did not know what to say to help them.

This realization of a profound lack of spirituality was a first step on the road to change. He now tried to reform his life and began to urge his congregation to lead moral lives. He started praying four times a day, a practice he would continue after his conversion. But as he later admitted, all of this was but an earnest 'working out a righteousness of his own', in which he tried to balance the sins of his life with good deeds. He actually kept a volume, in which he would record his sins on one page and his good deeds on another, with the hope that at year's end they would balance. Although accurate dating is not possible, it seems he went on like this for seven years, from 1734 to 1741. Sometimes, though, the futility of trying to find salvation through the pathway of good works would overwhelm him and he would despair. Once he actually cried out in the middle of a service: 'My friends, we are in a damnable state, and I scarcely know how we are to get out of it'. He was beginning to realize, in the words of the Methodist historian Frank Baker, that 'he could not put himself right with God by a multitude of devotional exercises, however arduous'.

During this period of time, in 1735, Grimshaw was married to a widow named Sarah Sutcliffe, whom he loved dearly, but who, after bearing him two children, died at the very young age of twenty-nine. Grimshaw was shattered. He went through months of deep depression—not only mourning for his wife but also sorrowing over his sinful state. He was harassed with sexual temptations, which he resisted, but which left him deeply troubled. Old Deistic notions reappeared. On one occasion, for example, he 'was tempted to believe Christ to be but a mere man.' On another, the thought entered his mind that the God of the Bible was 'a cruel implacable Being.'

But in the midst of his despair God sent him deliverance through, among other things, the agency of a book. The book was *The Doctrine of Justification by Faith Through the Imputation of the Righteousness of Christ, Explained, Confirmed, & Vindicated* by the Puritan divine John Owen. Visiting a friend in 1741, Grimshaw happened to see the book lying on a table. Seeing from the title on the spine that it was a theological work, he picked it up and went to open it to the title page. Then, a strange event happened. As he was opening the book he felt 'an uncommon heat' flush his face. Thinking that the flash of heat must have come from a fire in the fireplace of the room, he turned towards it but realized that it was too far away to have caused the flash of heat. He opened the book again and experienced a second heat flash. He took these flashes of heat to be divine signs that this book would be of special help to him. And so it proved.

In this classic study of the imputed righteousness of Christ, Owen argued that justification meant that the sinner who was justified no longer sought to commend himself to God through his own good deeds, but rested in the fact that the righteousness of Christ was reckoned to him, giving him a spotless holiness purer than an angel's. Reading Owen, Grimshaw was enabled, as he later put it, to 'renounce myself, every degree of fancied merit and ability, and to embrace Christ only for my all in all. O what light and comfort did I now enjoy in my own soul, and what a taste of the pardoning love of God!' Grimshaw would become a key leader in the Revival and also a good friend of Whitefield.

THE DECLINE OF DISSENT

Part of the reason for this spiritual ineffectiveness of the ministers of the Church of England is the fact that in the year 1662 around two thousand ministers of the Church of England, the most spiritually-minded group in the established Church at the time, had been expelled from her ranks for refusing to conform completely to the rites and practices of the Church of England. These men, known to history as the Puritans, had sought unsuccessfully for close to a hundred years to bring reform and renewal to the Church of England. Eventually they were forced out to join three fledgling denominations: about 1,700 ministers ended up as English Presbyterians; some 180 became Congregationalists; and a handful joined the Particular Baptists, also known as the Calvinistic Baptists. These three groups became known as the 'Dissenters' or 'Nonconformists'. Little wonder then that the Church of

England found herself at a distinct spiritual disadvantage when it came to leading the nation in moral and spiritual reform in the early eighteenth century.

But even among many of the churches of the Dissenters, the children of the Puritans, things were little better. As early as the 1670s, some Puritan leaders were concerned about the low spiritual state of both themselves and their congregations. For example, in 1678, the Puritan preacher John Howe delivered a series of sermons based on Ezekiel 39:29 in which he dealt with the subject of the outpouring of the Holy Spirit. In one of these sermons he told his audience:

> When the Spirit shall be poured forth plentifully I believe you will hear much other kind of sermons, or they will, who shall live to such a time, than you are wont to do now-a-days ... It is plain, too sadly plain, there is a great retraction of the Spirit of God even from us; we not know how to speak living sense [*i.e. felt reality*] unto souls, how to get within you; our words die in our mouths, or drop and die between you and us. We even faint, when we speak; long experienced unsuccessfulness makes us despond; we speak not as persons that hope to prevail ... When such an effusion of the Spirit shall be as is here signified ... [*ministers*] shall know how to speak to better purpose, with more compassion and sense, with more seriousness, with more authority and allurement, than we now find we can.

By the time that Whitefield was born in 1714, many of the children of the Puritans were conscious of their spiritual weakness. One knowledgeable observer of the churches of the Dissenters bemoaned the fact that 'the distinguished doctrines of the gospel—Christ crucified, the only ground of hope for fallen man—salvation through his atoning blood—the sanctification by his eternal Spirit, are old-fashioned things now seldom heard in our churches'. The Christian life was basically defined in terms of a moral life of good works. Spiritual ardour was regarded with horror as 'enthusiasm' or fanaticism. The ideal of the era is well summed up by an inscription on a tombstone from the period: 'pious without enthusiasm'.

The spiritual situation in which early eighteenth-century Dissenters thus found themselves is well described by two Congregationalist ministers in 1737, Isaac Watts, the father of the English hymn, and John Guyse. 'There has been a great and just complaint for many years', they wrote, 'that the work of conversion goes on very slowly, that the Spirit of God in his saving influences is much withdrawn from the ministrations of his word, and there are few that receive the report of the gospel, with any eminent success upon their hearts'. They were thus constrained to pray, 'Return, O Lord, and visit thy churches, and revive thine own work in the midst of us'. God would answer this prayer—but not at all in the way they expected, for revival would first come to the Church of England, and from her flame, it would spread to the Dissenters.

3

SEEKING CHRIST

THE HOLY CLUB

George Whitefield was the youngest son of Thomas Whitefield, the proprietor of the Bell Inn, the finest hotel in Gloucester. George's father died when he was but two and so he was raised by his mother Elizabeth. His school record was unremarkable, save for a noticeable talent for acting. For a while during his teen years, when his older brother Richard took over the running of the inn, he worked as one of the servants. But his mother longed for something better for her son. Her persistence and the kindness of friends enabled him in November 1732 to enter Pembroke College, Oxford University as a servitor (student servant). It was at Oxford the following summer that he first met John Wesley and his younger brother Charles, who were regularly meeting with a group of men known to history as 'the Holy Club'. This was a company of ten or so men who were ardently trying to live religious lives in an extremely dissolute age.

Whitefield, like-minded and longing for spiritual companionship ever since coming up to Oxford, joined them. He engaged in numerous religious exercises such as fasting, praying regularly, attending public worship, and seeking to abstain from what were deemed worldly pleasures. Systematic reading of Puritan and Pietist books of spirituality also occupied much of Whitefield's time. Despite the evident zeal he brought to these religious activities he had no sense of peace with God or that God was satisfied with what he was doing. He was, though he did not know it at the time, treading a pathway similar to the one that Martin Luther had taken over two hundred years earlier. And just as Luther's conversion was the spark that lit the fires of the Reformation, so Whitefield's conversion would be central to kindling the blaze of the eighteenth-century Evangelical Revival.

Conversion came in the spring of 1735 after Charles Wesley had given him a copy of *The Life of God in the Soul of Man* (1677) by Henry Scougal, a one-time Professor of Divinity at Aberdeen. This book was a frontal challenge to Whitefield's ardent endeavour to create a righteous life that would merit God's favour. Here is the way Whitefield recalled it many years later in a sermon that he preached in 1769:

> I must bear testimony to my old friend Mr. Charles Wesley, he put a book into my hands, called, The Life of God in the Soul of Man, whereby God showed me, that I must be born again, or be damned. I know the place: it may be superstitious, perhaps, but whenever I go to Oxford, I cannot help running to that

*place where Jesus Christ first revealed himself to me, and gave
me the new birth. As a good writer [i.e. Scougal] says, a man
may go to church, say his prayers, receive the Sacrament, and
yet, my brethren, not be a Christian. How did my heart rise,
how did my heart shudder, like a poor man that is afraid to look
into his account-books, lest he should find himself a bankrupt:
yet shall I burn that book, shall I throw it down, shall I put
it by, or shall I search into it? I did [search it], and, holding
the book in my hand, thus addressed the God of heaven and
earth: Lord, if I am not a Christian, if I am not a real one, for
Jesus Christ's sake, show me what Christianity is, that I may
not be damned at last. I read a little further, and the cheat
was discovered; O, says the author, they that know any thing
of religion know it is a vital union with the Son of God, Christ
formed in the heart; O what a ray of divine life did then break
in upon my poor soul ...*

Awakened by this book to his need for the new birth,
Whitefield passionately struggled to find salvation along
the pathway of extreme asceticism but to no avail. Finally,
when he had come to an end of his resources as a human
being, God enabled him, in his words, 'to lay hold on his
dear Son by a living faith, and, by giving me the Spirit of
adoption, to seal me, as I humbly hope, even to the day of
everlasting redemption.' And, he went on, 'oh! with what
joy—joy unspeakable—even joy that was full of, and big
with glory, was my soul filled ... '

EARLY MINISTRY AND AMERICA
Whitefield was ordained deacon in Gloucester Cathedral
in June of 1736, and graduated from Oxford the following

month. That summer he preached his first sermon in the
Church of St. Mary de Crypt, where he had been baptized
as an infant. Between his ordination as deacon and his
death thirty-four years later, his younger contemporary
Augustus Montague Toplady calculated that Whitefield
gave an estimated 18,000 sermons. Actually, if one includes
all of the talks that he gave, he probably spoke about an
amazing thousand times a year during his ministry. Many
of these sermons were delivered to massive congregations
that numbered 10,000 or so, with some audiences possibly
as large as 30,000. Though such numbers sound like
puffery to contemporary readers, recent study by Braxton
Boren, a Ph.D. candidate in acoustic archaeology, has
demonstrated that it was entirely possible for Whitefield's
voice to have been heard by such crowds.

Two years after his ordination, he sailed to Georgia
at the urging of Charles Wesley, who had spent some
months there in 1736. It was on this initial foray to
America that Whitefield conceived the idea of founding
an orphanage in Georgia, which would involve him raising
significant amounts of money to keep it going over the
rest of his career. He returned to Britain that same year
to be ordained priest in Oxford the following January. A
preaching tour through England followed from February to
April, 1739, in which Whitefield developed two key aspects
of his future ministry: totally extemporaneous sermons and
open-air preaching. The latter became part of his ministry
arsenal when his preaching began to arouse opposition and
pulpits began to be closed to him.

At his first open-air service in February of 1739 on the outskirts of Bristol there were 200 people or so, nearly all of them miners from the Kingswood collieries. Within six weeks or so, Whitefield was preaching numerous times a week to crowds sometimes numbering in the thousands! Whitefield's description of his ministry at this time is a classic one. To visualize the scene, we need to picture the green countryside, the piles of coal, the squalid huts, and the unwashed faces of the colliers as we read his words:

Having no righteousness of their own to renounce, they were glad to hear of a Jesus who was a friend of publicans, and came not to call the righteous, but sinners to repentance. The first discovery of their being affected was to see the white gutters made by their tears which plentifully fell down their black cheeks, as they came out of their coal pits. Hundreds and hundreds of them were soon brought under deep convictions, which, as the event proved, happily ended in a sound and thorough conversion. The change was visible to all, though numbers chose to impute it to anything, rather than the finger of God.

Here is another description from this same period of time, when others besides the miners of Bristol were flocking to hear Whitefield preach:

As ... I had just begun to be an extempore preacher, it often occasioned many inward conflicts. Sometimes, when twenty thousand people were before me, I had not, in my own apprehension, a word to say either to God or them. But I never was totally deserted, and frequently ... so assisted, that I knew by happy experience what our Lord meant by saying, 'Out of his belly shall flow rivers of living water' (John 7:38). The open firmament above me, the prospect of the adjacent fields, with the sight of thousands and thousands, some in coaches, some on horseback, and some in the trees, and at times all affected and drenched in tears together, to which sometimes was added the solemnity of the approaching evening, was almost too much for, and quite overcame me.

Before a second trip to America in the late summer of 1739, Whitefield had begun preaching to the huge crowds that made him a celebrity throughout the British Empire. Revival had come to England! And to that revival, and its confluent streams in Wales, Scotland, and British North America no man contributed more than Whitefield. The Anglican evangelist was a remarkable preacher. The great Shakespearian actor David Garrick, who was averse to bombast, deeply admired Whitefield for his elocutionary abilities. Even the irreligious philosopher David Hume is reported to have said that Whitefield 'was worth going twenty miles to hear'. As the following chapters will unfold, Whitefield also had a solid grasp of theology and biblical truth—his pulpit ministry was not mere show.

Yet, Whitefield was not averse to using various strategies to promote his ministry. In the early days he travelled with William Seward, who had made a fortune as a stock-broker before his conversion in 1738 through the witness of Charles Wesley. Of his conversion Seward later wrote in his journal:

I cannot sufficiently praise God for bringing me out of that darkness into his marvellous light ... This is a faith I never really felt before Mr. Charles Wesley expounded it to me. I cannot but always honour him as an instrument in God's hand for showing me the true way of salvation by Jesus Christ.

Seward was a consummate publicist, fundraiser and organizer, who helped Whitefield enormously on his second trip to America by publicizing his ministry in American newspapers and so creating a desire in the readers to see this remarkable preacher. Sadly Seward died as a result of a large rock being thrown at the back of his head while he was preaching in Hay-on-Wye in Wales in the autumn of 1740.

THE GRAND ITINERANT

In addition to his preaching throughout the length and breadth of England, Whitefield regularly itinerated throughout Wales, where he built strong friendships with leading Welsh Evangelicals Howel Harris and Daniel Rowland. He visited Ireland three times and journeyed fourteen times to Scotland. He crossed the Atlantic thirteen times, stopping once in Bermuda for eleven weeks, and preached in virtually every major town on the Atlantic seaboard—he was in America in 1738, 1739–1741, 1744–1748, 1751–1752, 1754–1755, 1763–1765, and finally 1769–1770. What is so remarkable about all of this is Whitefield lived at a time when travel to a town but twenty miles away was a significant undertaking. In all of his voyages to America Whitefield spent a total of two years or so on the Atlantic; as he once described himself, he was 'an amphibious itinerant'. Others, however, called him 'the grand itinerant'.

In journeying to Scotland and to America he was going to what many perceived as the fringes of transatlantic British society and culture. And yet some of God's richest blessings on his ministry was in these very regions. Commenting on Whitefield's impact on America, American historian Harry Stout has noted that so pervasive was Whitefield's impact in America that he can justly be styled America's first cultural hero. Before Whitefield, there was no unifying intercolonial person or event. Indeed, before Whitefield, it is doubtful any name other than royalty was known equally from Boston to Charleston. But by 1750 virtually every American loved and admired Whitefield and saw him as their champion.

REVIVAL IN NEW ENGLAND

Whitefield's second trip to America from 1739 to 1741 played a central role in what historians of American Christianity call the First Great Awakening. After ministry in the southern colonies, Whitefield arrived in New England in mid-September 1740. His coming long anticipated by many of the New England ministers, he quickly threw himself into a breathtaking round of itinerant preaching. In Boston and its neighbourhood, where he preached for twenty-six days, the response to his ministry was overwhelming. His farewell sermon on Boston Common on October 12, for instance, drew more than twenty thousand listeners according to Benjamin Franklin, the largest crowd ever assembled in America to that point in history. Estimates of those converted between 1740 and 1742 in New England alone, where the population was around 250,000 at the time, range from 25,000 to 50,000. These figures, it should be noted, do not include conversions of those who were already church members.

In the middle of the revival William Cooper, the Congregationalist minister of Brattle Street Church, Boston, gave his perspective on what God was doing in his day.

The dispensation of grace we are now under, is certainly such as neither we nor our fathers have seen; and in some circumstances so wonderful, that I believe there has not been the like since the extraordinary pouring out of the Spirit immediately after our Lord's ascension. The apostolical times seem to have returned upon us: such a display has there been of the power and grace of the divine Spirit in the assemblies of his people, and such testimonies has he given to the word of the gospel. ... A number of preachers have appeared among us, to whom God has given such a large measure of his Spirit, that we are ready sometimes to apply to them the character given of Barnabas, that 'he was a good man, and full of the Holy Ghost, and of faith' [Acts 11:24]. They preach the gospel of the grace of God from place to place, with uncommon zeal and assiduity. The doctrines they insist on are the doctrines of the Reformation, under the influence whereof the power of godliness so flourished in the last century. The points on which their preaching mainly turns are those important ones of man's guilt, corruption, and impotence; supernatural regeneration by the Spirit of God, and free justification by faith in the righteousness of Christ; and the marks of the new birth. The manner of their preaching is not with the 'enticing words of man's wisdom' [1 Corinthians 2:4]; howbeit, they 'speak wisdom among them that are perfect' [1 Corinthians 2:6]. An ardent love to Christ and souls warms their breasts and animates their labours. God has made those his ministers active spirits, a flame of fire in his service; and his word in their mouths has been, 'as a fire, and as a hammer that breaketh the rock in pieces' [Jeremiah 23:29].

Here Cooper placed the revival in New England within the broad sweep of church history. He was utterly convinced that no other revival, in either his lifetime or that of his Puritan forebears, was comparable to what God was doing in the early 1740s. In some respects only at the time of Pentecost could one find something genuinely comparable! The preaching through which God had brought about this revival, though, did not contain anything new. Essentially it was the same doctrine of salvation that was trumpeted forth at the time of the Reformation and in the Puritan era, one that highlighted humanity's total depravity, the Spirit's glorious sovereignty in regenerating sinners, and their justification by faith alone in Christ. And the preaching style fitted the doctrine: it was plain and ardent.

Cooper then went on to specify what he considered so extraordinary about the revival. First, there was the incredible way that it had swept through 'some of the most populous towns, the chief places of concourse and business'. Then, there were the numbers who had professed conversion: 'stupid sinners have been awakened by hundreds'. During the winter of 1740–1741 in Boston alone, Cooper stated, there were 'some thousands under such religious impressions as they never felt before'. People of all ages, from the very elderly to the very young, had been saved: the elderly 'snatched as brands out of the burning, made monuments of divine mercy' and 'sprightly youth ... made to bow like willows to the Redeemer's sceptre'. Moreover, God had drawn to himself some of the grossest sinners in New England: drunkards, fornicators and adulterers, people addicted to profanity and 'carnal worldlings have been made to seek first the kingdom of God and his righteousness'. On the other hand, many of those who deemed themselves upright and moral have become convinced that 'morality is not to be relied on for life; and so excited to seek after the new birth, and a vital union to Jesus Christ by faith'. And at the heart of this remarkable awakening was George Whitefield and his preaching.

WHITEFIELD MEETS JONATHAN EDWARDS

In February of 1740, Jonathan Edwards, the premier theologian in America, had sat down at his desk to write a letter of invitation to George Whitefield, who was then in Georgia, to come and preach for his congregation in Northampton, Massachusetts, that summer. He had heard, he told Whitefield, that the English evangelist was 'one who has the blessing of heaven' attending him wherever he went and he hoped that 'such a blessing' might descend on Northampton, enter his house and even fill his own soul. 'It has been with refreshment of soul,'

Edwards continued, 'that I have heard of one raised up in the Church of England to revive the mysterious, spiritual, despised and exploded [that is, held in contempt] doctrines of the gospel, and full of a Spirit of zeal for the promotion of real, vital piety, whose labours have been attended with such success. Blessed be God that hath done it! Who is with you, and helps you, and makes the weapons of your warfare mighty'.

As we have noted, Whitefield actually did not get to New England until that autumn and to Northampton till October. Whitefield spent six days with Edwards, from Friday, October 17 to the following Wednesday, October 22. As he preached from the Northampton pulpit on the Sunday morning, Whitefield noted in his diary that 'Edwards wept during the whole time of exercise' and that the congregation were 'equally affected'. During the afternoon service, he recorded, 'the power increased yet more'. In all Whitefield spoke on five occasions in the town, and, Edwards later wrote in 1743, 'the congregation was extraordinarily melted by every sermon', with 'almost the whole assembly being in tears' during the preaching.

MARRIAGE AND LATER MINISTRY

If Edwards was deeply affected by Whitefield's preaching, the English evangelist was deeply impressed by Edwards and his wife Sarah as a couple. As he noted in his diary at the time:

Felt great satisfaction in being at the house of Mr. Edwards. A sweeter couple I have not yet seen ... Mrs. Edwards is adorned with a meek and quiet spirit; she talked solidly of the things of God, and seemed to be such a helpmeet for her husband, that she caused me to renew those prayers which, for some months, I have put up to God, that he would be pleased to send me a daughter of Abraham to be my wife.

Whitefield did find a wife upon his return to England in 1741 but his marriage was not at all like that of the Edwardses. A statement of Thomas Hooker, one of the key founders of Puritan New England, well expresses the essence of the Edwards' marriage: 'The man whose heart is endeared to the woman he loves, he dreams of her in the night, hath her in his eye and apprehension when he awakes, museth on her as he sits at table'. What thrilled Whitefield about his marriage to Elizabeth James of Abergavenny, Wales—to whom Howel Harris had been engaged and who gave her up so Whitefield could marry her—was that she would not attempt to hinder him in his calling as an itinerant evangelist! J. C. Ryle noted that 'his marriage does not seem to have contributed much to his happiness' and Cornelius Winter, who knew Whitefield well in his latter days, commented that he 'was not happy in his wife'.

The early 1740s also witnessed a division in the Revival between Whitefield and the Wesley brothers, John and Charles, who were maintaining that God bestowed a second blessing, as it were, which consisted of being free from sin in thought, word, and deed. Neither of the brothers ever claimed to have received this blessing personally, and Charles later in the 1760s openly questioned the biblical legitimacy of his brother's position on this matter. But in the early 1740s both Methodist leaders argued that as this doctrinal distinctive was preached, God honoured the preaching and gave the gift. Exacerbating the rift between Whitefield and the Wesleys was also the Wesleys' public criticism of Calvinism. Whitefield's thinking in both of these areas will be examined in subsequent chapters.

In 1741 Whitefield's friends in London built a wooden meeting-house for him that came to be called the Moorfields Tabernacle. In this way, he had a headquarters in the English capital and a ready place to preach. Twelve years later it was replaced by a brick structure. It was here that Robert Robinson, whose conversion will be discussed in Chapter 8, heard Whitefield preach on Matthew 3:7. Similar meeting-houses would be built for him in Bristol and Philadelphia in the 1750s. In 1756, he built a second meeting-house in London, in Tottenham Court Road, which soon became the largest Nonconformist Church in the world at that time.

By the early 1750s, the relationship between Whitefield and the Wesley brothers had been essentially repaired. It is noteworthy that a friendship between Charles' wife Sarah Gwynne Wesley and Selina Hastings, the Countess of Huntingdon, who had appointed Whitefield as one of her chaplains in 1748, played a role in the healing of this relationship. The Countess had been converted in the late 1730s and used her significant wealth to support not only Whitefield but a number of other preachers, who eventually seceded from the Church of England as the Countess of Huntingdon's Connexion in 1783.

During the 1750s and 1760s Whitefield continued to itinerate throughout the English-speaking transatlantic world as he had always done. But the pace was beginning to take its toll on his body. When he turned fifty in 1764, to many of his friends he seemed to be 'an old, old man'. And five years later, when John Wesley saw him in 1769, he thought he was close to death. And so it proved, for he passed away on his final trip to America in 1770, and was buried in Old South Church, Newburyport, Massachusetts.

4

TAKING THE WORD
OVER LAND AND SEA

PREACHING REFORMATION TRUTH

Whitefield was always an avid reader. A few months after his conversion, he began to prayerfully peruse the Puritan biblical commentaries of William Burkitt and Matthew Henry, both of whom had died at the beginning of the eighteenth century—Henry actually died the summer before Whitefield was born. These Puritan authors led to Whitefield becoming convinced of 'free grace and the necessity of being justified in His [i.e. God's] sight by *faith only*.' Following his ordination as deacon in the Church of England in 1736 these Reformation doctrines came to occupy a central place in his preaching arsenal. There is, for instance, an account of Whitefield's preaching drawn up by an unknown French contemporary. Dated August 1739, this observer states that Whitefield preaches 'continually about inner regeneration, the new birth in Jesus Christ, the movement of the Spirit, justification by faith through grace, the life of the Spirit'.

The following year Joseph Smith, a Congregationalist minister from Charleston, South Carolina, defended Whitefield against various attacks in *The Character, Preaching, etc. of the Rev. George Whitefield*. In the section dealing with the doctrinal content of Whitefield's sermons, Smith lists four 'primitive, protestant, puritanic' doctrines that Whitefield regularly heralded in his preaching in America—original sin, 'justification by faith alone', the new birth, and 'inward feelings of the Spirit'. Smith recalled the way in which Whitefield 'earnestly contended for our justification as the free gift of God, by faith alone in the blood of Christ, an article of faith delivered to the saints of old ... telling us plainly, and with the clearest distinction, that a man was justified these three ways; meritoriously by Christ, instrumentally by faith alone, declaratively by good works'.

AN OPEN-AIR PREACHER

Given the spiritual, intellectual and moral climate of England in Whitefield's day, which we looked at in chapter 2, it is not surprising that his preaching on the new birth was not well received by the Anglican clergy in England, and churches began to be barred to him. Whitefield, however, was not to be deterred. As we saw in the last chapter, on Saturday, February 17, 1739, Whitefield made the decision to take to the open air and preach to a group of colliers in Kingswood, a coal-mining district on the outskirts of Bristol. These men with their families lived in squalor and utter degradation, squandering their lives in drink and violence. With no church nearby, they were quite ignorant of Christianity and its leading tenets. It was a key turning-point in not only his life but also in the history of Evangelicalism. The concern that has gripped evangelicals in the last two hundred years to bring the gospel message directly to ordinary people has some of its most significant roots here in Whitefield's venturing out to preach in the open air. For much of the nineteenth and twentieth centuries, Whitefield's innovative role in this regard was forgotten, but recent publications, especially that of Arnold Dallimore's two-volume life of Whitefield, have certainly gone far in redressing this amnesia.

From this point on Whitefield would relish and delight in his calling as an open-air preacher. He would preach in fields and foundries, in ships, cemeteries, and pubs, atop horses and even coffins, from stone walls and balconies, staircases and windmills. As a divine example, he would cite Christ's public ministry, who, according to Whitefield in his sermon *What think ye of Christ?* (1739), 'preached on a mount, in a ship, and a field.' Years later, he noted how he still loved preaching in the open air. For instance, in a letter dated December 14, 1768, he wrote, 'I love the open bracing air'. And the following year he could state: 'It is good to go into the high-ways and hedges. Field-preaching, field-preaching for ever!'

It should be noted that Whitefield never confined his witnessing about Christ to preaching occasions. He took every opportunity to share his faith. 'God forbid', he once remarked, 'I should travel with anybody a quarter of an hour without speaking of Christ to them'. On another occasion, during his sixth preaching tour of America, he happened to stay with a wealthy, though worldly, family in Southold on Long Island. The family discovered after the evangelist had left their home that he had written with a diamond on one of the windowpanes in the bedroom where he had slept, 'One thing is needful'!

It also bears noting that Whitefield's sermons were not tremendously long. As he said in the preface to the hymnal that he designed for use at the Tabernacle: 'I am no great friend to long sermons, long prayers, or long hymns'. Cornelius Winter, who travelled with him in the last phase of his ministry in the 1760s, noted that normally before he preached he would spend an hour or two in prayer and meditation and that many of his best sermons were preached first thing in the morning around six o'clock. Winter also noted that he never once heard Whitefield stumble or hesitate over a word while preaching. He always seemed to have complete command of his subject.

ACCUSED OF FANATICISM

Whitefield's ministry—insisting, as it did, on the vital necessity of conversion and the work of the Holy Spirit in the heart—was not without its critics, many of whom castigated him for what they regarded as fanaticism. In an interview with John Wesley on August 18, 1739, for example, Joseph Butler, the Bishop of Bristol, accused both Wesley and Whitefield of 'pretending to extraordinary revelations and gifts of the Holy Ghost', which he found 'a horrid thing—a very horrid thing'. Of course, if Whitefield had been present, he would have rightly disputed the accuracy of Butler's accusation. John Callender, a Baptist pastor in Newport, Rhode Island, denounced Whitefield as 'a second George Fox', obviously convinced, and wrongly so, that Whitefield, like the founder of the Quakers, publicly promoted the restoration of the extraordinary gifts of the Holy Spirit.

It should be admitted that in his early ministry Whitefield did make some unguarded statements and adopted certain attitudes that helped fuel this opposition. On his second preaching tour of America, for instance, Whitefield appears to have maintained that assurance belonged to the essence of saving faith and that a mature Christian could discern the marks of conversion in another individual. As Jonathan Dickinson, the first president of the College of New Jersey (later known as Princeton University) and a friend to the revival, remarked about Whitefield's views at this time: 'I cannot stand surety for all his sentiments in religion, particularly his making assurance to be essentially necessary to a justifying faith; And his openly declaring for a spirit of discerning in experienced Christians, whereby they can know who are true converts, and who are close hypocrites'. To his credit, Whitefield would later admit his injudiciousness and that he had been far 'too rash and hasty' in his speech and published writings. 'Wild-fire has been mixed with it', he wrote in 1748, 'and I find that I frequently wrote and spoke in my own spirit, when I thought I was writing and speaking by the assistance of the Spirit of God'. Despite these faults—basically overcome by his early thirties— multitudes of Whitefield's hearers found his preaching 'moving, earnest, winning, melting' and rooted in a doctrinal framework which, in the words of Thomas Prince, a New England pastor and historian, was 'plainly that of the Reformers'.

In the early years of the revival Whitefield's itinerant, open-air preaching was often paraded as evidence of his 'enthusiasm', or fanaticism. Part of Whitefield's response to this criticism was to go back to the example of the Apostle Paul as found in the Book of Acts. 'Was he not filled', he asked his opponents, 'with a holy restless Impatience and insatiable Thirst of travelling, and undertaking dangerous Voyages for the Conversion of Infidels ... ?' Here Whitefield lays before us the spiritual passion that spurred his own incessant travelling over land and sea: the longing to see sinners embrace Christ as Lord and Saviour and find their deepest spiritual thirst and hunger satisfied in Christ alone.

CRITICIZED BY THE ERSKINE BROTHERS
Criticism of the wide-ranging nature of his ministry also came from such ardent Evangelicals as Ebenezer Erskine and his younger brother Ralph, founders of the Secession Church in Scotland. This body of churches had seceded from the Scottish national church in the 1730s over the issue of whether or not the people of a congregation had the right to refuse a minister chosen for them by the

Presbytery or heritors (i.e. landowners who possessed hereditary rights to property within a parish). The Erskines had invited Whitefield to preach solely in their churches. But Whitefield refused to be pinned down to a few locales and insisted on preaching wherever he was given a pulpit in Scotland. He told the Erskines that he was 'more and more determined to go out into the highways and hedges; and that if the Pope himself would lend me his pulpit, I would gladly proclaim the righteousness of Jesus Christ therein.'

That Whitefield failed to understand the concern of the Erskines for the reformation of the church is evident in the sad disagreement between them. Yet, his reply well reveals his passion for the salvation of the lost wherever they might be. As he told a Scottish nobleman, Lord Rae, a few days after this discussion with the Erskines, the 'full desire' of his soul was to 'see the kingdom of God come with power'. He was, he went on, 'determined to seek after and know nothing else. For besides this, all other things are but dung and dross'. Still in Scotland two months later, the same spiritual desire still deeply gripped him. 'I want a thousand tongues to set off the Redeemer's praise', he told the Earl of Leven and Melville.

THE CAUSE OF HIS EVANGELISTIC PASSION

What was the passion that ignited this evangelistic ministry of Whitefield? Well, first of all, there was his love for God and his concern for the glory of the triune God. As he told John Harvey Sweetland on February 21, 1738: 'I wish I had 1000 lives that I might offer them all for God, for indeed ... he is worthy of them all.' And in his sermon *What think ye of Christ?* (1739), Whitefield told his hearers, 'if we can assure our consciences, before God, that we act with a single eye to his glory, we are cheerfully to go on in our work, and not in the least to regard what men or devils can say against, or do unto us.' Fifteen years later, he declared: 'Was it not sinful, I could wish for a thousand hands, a thousand tongues, and a thousand lives: all should be employed night and day, without ceasing, in promoting the glory of the ever-lovely, ever-loving Jesus.'

Then, there was Whitefield's love for the lost. On his third preaching tour of America in the mid-1740s, he told Joshua Gee, one of his correspondents, 'Oh that I was a flame of pure & holy fire, & had [a] thousand lives to Spend in the dear Redeemers service', for the 'sight of so many perishing Souls every day affects me much, & makes me long to go if possible from Pole to Pole, to proclaim redeeming love'. 'Had I a thousand souls and bodies', he noted in 1753, 'they should be all itinerants for Jesus Christ.' For Whitefield, 'the main end' of his calling as a minister was, as it once put it, 'the recovery and saving of souls.'

In 1747, he told a correspondent that because 'Jesus hath of late remarkably appeared for me',

> I ought to lay myself out more and more in going about endeavouring to do good to precious and immortal souls. At present this is my settled resolution. The Redeemer seems to approve of it; for the fields in the Southern parts are white ready unto harvest, and many seem to have the hearing ear.

All next October, God willing, I have devoted to poor North Carolina. It is pleasant hunting in the woods after the lost sheep for whom the Redeemer hath shed his precious blood. May the Lord of the harvest spirit up more to go forth in his strength, to compel poor sinners to come in!

One of the best places to see this love in action is to read the close of so many of his sermons, where he would plead with the lost to heed the call to salvation that God had made through his lips. In 1844, John Knight, an elderly man of eighty-one, recalled the time that he had heard Whitefield preach on the evangelist's final visit to Gloucestershire in 1769. According to Knight, he was 'about 6 years of age' at the time. 'My father held me up in his arms,' he wrote, 'and though so young I well remember to have seen the tears run down the cheek of that Servant of God while preaching the love of his Master to dying sinners.'

GOD BLESSING THE PREACHED WORD
Nothing gave Whitefield greater joy than to report to his friends that God was blessing his preaching. 'The word runs and is glorified,' a line from Paul's second letter to the Thessalonians (2 Thessalonians 3:1), and Jesus' statement to his disciples that the fields were 'white already to harvest' (John 4:35) were frequent refrains in his correspondence. Writing from Pennsylvania in May of 1746, Whitefield informed a correspondent in Gloucestershire, England, that Christ 'gives me full employ on this side the water, & causes his word to run & be glorified ... Everywhere the fields are white ready unto harvest. I am just now

going to tell lost sinners that there is yet room for them in the side of Jesus'. Upon hearing of the marriage of one of his nephews in 1756, Whitefield observed, 'Alas, what a changing world do we live in! Blessed be God for an unchangeable Christ! Amidst all, this is my comfort, his word runs and is glorified'. Christ 'vouchsafes daily (O amazing love) to own my feeble labours', he told a friend in 1757. Then he added: 'The word runs and is glorified'. Or writing in 1768 to a fellow minister in Scotland: 'In London the word runs and is glorified, and in Edinburgh, I trust, the prospect is promising. The fields are white ready unto harvest'.

THE CONVERSION OF THOMAS OLIVERS

Another vantage–point from which to view Whitefield's ministry of the Word is to look at the impact of his preaching on various individuals. Let us consider two, both of them writers of verse. First, Thomas Olivers, the Welsh Methodist who was later closely associated with the Wesleys and the author of the well–known hymn 'The God of Abraham praise'. Notorious for his addiction to foul swearing and in his own words, 'one of the most profligate and abandoned young men living,' Olivers went to hear Whitefield preach in Bristol in 1748. The evangelist's text was Zechariah 3:2: 'Is not this a brand plucked out of the fire?' When Whitefield began his sermon, Olivers said,

> I was certainly a dreadful enemy to God and to all that is good, ... but by the time it was ended I was become a new creature. For, in the first place, I was deeply convinced of the great goodness of God towards me all my life, particularly

in that he had given his Son to die for me. I had also a far
clearer view of all my sins, particularly my base ingratitude
towards him. These discoveries quite broke my heart, and
caused showers of tears to trickle down my cheeks. I was
likewise filled with an utter abhorrence of my evil ways, and was
much ashamed that ever I had walked in them. And as my heart
was thus turned from all evil, so it was powerfully inclined to all
that is good. It is not easy to express what strong desires I had
for God and his service, and what resolutions I had to seek and
serve him in future; in consequence of which I broke off all my
evil practices, and forsook all my wicked and foolish companions
without delay, and gave myself up to God and his service with
my whole heart.

The first Sunday after his conversion Olivers was up early
to attend the six a.m. worship service at Bristol Cathedral.
During it, he later said, 'I felt as I had done with earth,
and was praising God! No words can set forth the joy, the
rapture, the awe, and reverence I felt.'

THE WITNESS OF PHILLIS WHEATLEY

Now, listen to Phillis Wheatley, brought as a slave to
America from her native Gambia or Senegal when she
was seven. Sold in Boston to a merchant by the name of
John Wheatley, he named her Phillis after the slave ship
in which she was transported to America. Encouraged to
write poetry by John and his wife Susanna, she eventually
became the first published African-American poetess. In
an elegy for Whitefield, written after his death, she recalls
the impact that his preaching had on her as an African
Christian. She may well have heard Whitefield preach in

Boston's Old South Church, where she was baptized on
August 18, 1771. Whitefield had preached there three times
exactly a year before in August, 1770, only a few weeks
before his death. What is striking about her representation
of Whitefield's preaching is his concern for all of his
hearers, Americans of both European and African descent:

> He pray'd that grace in every heart might dwell:
> He long'd to see *America* excell;
> He charg'd its youth to let the grace divine
> Arise, and in their future actions shine;
> He offer'd *that* he did himself receive,
> A greater gift not *God* himself can give:
> He urg'd the need of *Him* to every one;
> It was no less than *God*'s co-equal *Son*!
> Take *Him* ye wretched for your only good;
> Take *Him* ye starving souls to be your food.
> Ye thirsty, come to his life giving stream:
> Ye Preachers, take him for your joyful theme:
> Take *Him*, 'my dear *Americans*,' he said,
> Be your complaints in his kind bosom laid:
> Take *Him* ye *Africans*, he longs for you;
> Impartial *Saviour*, is his title due;
> If you will chuse to walk in grace's road,
> You shall be sons, and kings, and priests to *God*.

5

BEING BORN AGAIN AND
JUSTIFIED BY FAITH ALONE

The Hanoverian Church of England, due to its moralism and worldliness described above in Chapter 1, was basically helpless when it came to dealing with the moral decline of England during the early eighteenth century. 'Morality of itself', as Whitefield once observed, 'will never carry us to heaven'. In making this point, Whitefield knew that he was attacking a key point of error in his day. The 'sum and substance of modern divinity', he once noted, is that people seek to live moral lives and 'then they ... accept of Jesus Christ to make up the deficiencies of their righteousness'. But this was to essentially to rob Christ of his glory as Saviour. Rather, it was the Revival's message of the new birth and justification by faith alone, both freely given by God without human merit, which Whitefield trumpeted forth throughout his life and which brought positive change and hope.

THE NEW BIRTH

Whitefield's thoughts about the new birth are well seen in a letter to Louise Sophie von der Schulenburg, the Countess of Delitz. The Countess was the illegitimate daughter of George I by one of his mistresses, Melusina von der Schulenburg, the Countess of Kendal. The Countess of Delitz was also a friend of Selina Hastings, the Countess of Huntingdon, and she appears to have been converted through Whitefield's ministry at either Selina's London apartment or Chelsea residence. Writing to the Countess of Delitz from Plymouth in February of 1749, Whitefield rejoices in her conversion.

Blessed be the God and Father of our Lord Jesus Christ, who, I trust, hath imparted a saving knowledge of his eternal Son to your Ladyship's heart. Your letter bespeaks the language of a soul which hath tasted that the Lord is gracious, and hath been initiated into the divine life. Welcome, thrice welcome, honoured Madam, into the world of new creatures! O what a scene of happiness lies before you! Your frames, my Lady, like the moon, will wax and wane; but the Lord Jesus, on whose righteousness you solely depend, will, notwithstanding, remain your faithful friend in heaven. Your Ladyship seems to have the right point in view, to get a constant abiding witness and indwelling of the blessed Spirit of God in your heart. This the Redeemer has purchased for you. Of this he has given your Ladyship a taste; this, I am persuaded, he will yet impart so plentifully to your heart, that out of it shall flow rivers of living waters. This Jesus spake of the Spirit, which they that believe on him should receive. As you have, therefore, honoured Madam, received the Lord Jesus, so walk in him even by faith. Lean on your beloved, and you shall go on comfortably through this howling wilderness, till you arrive at those blissful regions,

Where pain, and sin, and sorrow cease,
And all is calm, and joy, and peace.

The new birth entails a 'saving knowledge' of the Lord Jesus Christ that is far more than simple factual knowledge. It marries belief in him as the 'eternal Son' of God to trust in him as one's Redeemer from sin and its punishment. It means that one's trust for acceptance by God is no longer focused on one's own moral achievements but upon what God has done through Christ's spotless life, propitiatory death and resurrection. As Whitefield wrote on another occasion to a different correspondent: 'I hope you take particular care to beat down self-righteousness, and exalt the Lord Jesus alone in your hearts. I find, the only happiness is to lie down as a poor sinner at the feet of the once crucified, but now exalted Lamb of God, who died for our sins and rose again for our justification.'

Moreover, the new birth is intimately bound up with the gift of the Spirit. Those who experience the new birth are 'initiated into the divine life' as the Spirit comes to dwell in their hearts. This new birth ultimately comes from God. Only he can graciously enable a person to look to Christ alone for salvation. As Whitefield put it in the sermon

What think ye of Christ?, 'our salvation is all of God, from the beginning to the end.'

Finally, it is the new birth alone that sets a person on the road to heaven. In a sermon that he preached on Ephesians 4:24, Whitefield put this final point more bluntly: 'unless you are new creatures, you are in a state of damnation ... I tell thee, O man; I tell thee, O woman, whoever thou art, thou art a dead man, thou art a dead woman, nay a damned man, a damned woman, without a new heart.'

THE ERROR OF BAPTISMAL REGENERATION

Understandably Whitefield was critical of the doctrine of baptismal regeneration, prevalent in many quarters of the Church of England and which he referred to more than once as 'that Diana of the present age'—an allusion to the riot in Ephesus over the threat that Christianity posed to the worship of the goddess Artemis or Diana (Acts 19:21–40). His earliest printed sermon, *The Nature and Necessity of our Regeneration or New Birth in Christ Jesus* (1737), was ardent and plain in its rejection of baptismal regeneration. It is 'beyond all contradiction', he argued, 'that comparatively but few of those that are "born of water", are "born of the Spirit" likewise; to use another spiritual way of speaking, many are baptized with water, which were never baptized with the Holy Ghost.' Regeneration is not automatically dispensed when water baptism takes place. Rather, a person must experience 'an inward change and purity of heart, and cohabitation of his [i.e. Christ's] Holy Spirit.' A genuine Christian is one 'whose baptism is that of the heart, in the Spirit, and not merely in the water, whose praise is not of man but of God.'

It is noteworthy that Whitefield was not afraid of turning the substance of this criticism against the Baptist emphasis on believer's baptism. Writing in the summer of 1741 to a Baptist correspondent in Georgia, he urged him:

> *I hope you will not think all is done, because you have been baptized and received into full communion. I know too many that 'make a Christ of their adult baptism', and rest in that, instead of the righteousness of the blessed Jesus. God forbid that you should so learn Christ. O my dear friend, seek after a settlement in our dear Lord, so that you may experience that life which is hid with Christ in God.*

JUSTIFICATION BY FAITH ALONE

Turning to the doctrine of justification, there is probably no better place to view Whitefield's thinking on this subject than his sermon on 1 Corinthians 1:30, *Christ, the Believer's Wisdom, Righteousness, Sanctification and Redemption.* It was written out early in 1741 while Whitefield was on board ship on his way home to England from Georgia. It appears, though, that he had preached it various times in the preceding months on what was his second visit to America. It was eventually published in Edinburgh in 1742, and subsequently came out in further editions in other cities in England and America.

After emphasizing that the blessing of justification is rooted in God's everlasting love, Whitefield deals with the first thing that is attributed to Christ, 'wisdom'. True wisdom, he argues, is not 'indulging the lust of the flesh', a reference to the open immorality and godlessness of his day. Nor is it found in the acquisitive 'adding house to house'. Neither is it merely intellectual knowledge, for 'learned men are not always wise'. Making the same point to students in New England Whitefield declared: 'Learning without piety, will only make you more capable of promoting the kingdom of Satan'.

What then is genuine wisdom? Well, first, Whitefield says and here he quotes an ancient Greek maxim, it is to 'know thyself'. What do the children of God need to know about themselves? Well, that before their conversion they were darkness, and now, they are light in the Lord (see Ephesians 5:8). They know something of their lost estate. They see that that 'all their righteousnesses are but as filthy rags; that there is no health in their souls; that they are poor and miserable, blind and naked'. And knowing themselves they know their need of a Saviour. This knowledge is basic and foundational to any biblical spirituality.

The type of self-knowledge that Whitefield is advocating also logically leads to the realization of the need for Christ as one's righteousness. Whitefield develops this thought in terms of Christ's active and passive obedience. By the former Christ fulfills the entirety of the law's righteous demands. This righteousness is imputed to the believer so that he or she now legally possesses the righteousness of Christ. 'Does sin condemn? Christ's righteousness delivers believers from the guilt of it'. By the latter, Christ passively bears the punishment for the elect's sins—he takes legal responsibility for them, so that God the Father blots out the transgressions of believers, 'the flaming sword of God's wrath ... is now removed'. The spiritual importance of this truth Whitefield later laid out in a letter he wrote to a friend in 1746: 'Blessed be his [i.e. Christ's] name if He lets you see more & more that in Him and in Him only you have Righteousness & strength. The more you are led to this foundation, the more solid will be your Superstructure of Gospel holiness'.

And the means of receiving these precious benefits of Christ's death? Faith alone—believers, Whitefield affirms in his sermon on 1 Corinthians 1:30, are 'enabled [by the Father] to lay hold on Christ by faith'. Whitefield clearly indicates that faith itself does not save the sinner—only Christ saves. Faith unites the sinner to the Saviour. Thus, faith, though a necessary means to salvation, is not itself the cause or ground of salvation. Elsewhere, Whitefield made this point thus: 'Faith is the instrument whereby the sinner received the redemption of Jesus Christ into his own soul.' And as Whitefield emphasizes in his sermon on the text from 1 Corinthians: 'Christ is *their* Saviour'. Little wonder then that Whitefield, employing the text of Romans 8, goes on to underline the fact that such genuine self-knowledge not only provides the foundation for a truly biblical spirituality but also gives that spirituality a tone of triumphant joy: 'O believers! ... rejoice in the Lord always'. Whitefield knew that when the biblical truth of justification is grasped and appropriated, a deep sense of joy and freedom from the burden of sin floods the heart and one's relationship with God is firmly anchored.

Whitefield has a number of ways of describing this reliance on Christ. In one letter he calls Christ 'the believer's *hollow square*'. This metaphor is drawn from the European battlefields of the eighteenth century, where armies would regularly form massed squares of infantry three or four rows deep for protection and consolidated strength. If a soldier were wounded his comrades would place him in the centre of the square, where he would be a lot safer than if he were behind a skirmishing line. 'If we keep close' in the square that is Christ, Whitefield continues with the thought of the metaphor, 'we are impregnable. Here only I find refuge. Garrisoned in this, I can bid defiance to men and devils'.

In another letter, he talks of Christ as the believer's 'asylum'. Christ's 'Wounds and precious Blood is a Sure Asylum & Place of Refuge in every Time of Trouble', he told a friend. In yet a third example, he speaks of Christ alone being able to fill the deepest caverns of the human heart: 'Happy they who have fled to Jesus Christ for refuge: they have a peace that the world cannot give. O that the pleasure-taking, trifling flatterer knew what it was! He would no longer feel such an empty void, such a dreadful chasm in the heart which nothing but the presence of God can fill'.

THE CENTRAL PLACE OF JUSTIFICATION

This Reformation truth of justification by faith alone held a central place not only in Whitefield's thought but also in that of other key leaders of the revival that swept the British Isles and British North America in the mid-18th century. In chapter 1, we saw how it was this truth that was central in William Grimshaw's conversion. Not surprisingly, a couple of decades after his conversion, when the London Evangelical William Romaine asked Grimshaw for a statement of his doctrinal convictions, Grimshaw stated the following with regard to Christ's imputed righteousness:

> ... this very righteousness is sufficient to redeem all mankind; but it only is, and will be imputed to every penitent, believing soul ... Glory be to God for free grace. No reason can be assigned for this; only He would have mercy; because He would have mercy. ... in this righteousness, every member of Christ stands, and will stand, complete, irreprovable, and acceptable in God's sight, both at death and judgment.

Or consider a hymn of Augustus Montague Toplady, who was converted in a barn in Ireland listening to a Methodist lay preacher expound a text from Ephesians 2. Subsequently he became the minister of the parish of Broad-Hembury, Devonshire, in 1768. It was here he composed his famous hymn, 'Rock of Ages, cleft for me,' which has been described by historian Horton Davies as essentially a poetic and 'powerful expression of the doctrine and experience of justification by faith.'

Rock of ages, cleft for me,
Let me hide myself in thee;
Let the water and the blood
From thy riven side which flow'd
Be of sin the double cure,
Cleanse me from its guilt and pow'r.

Not the labours of my hands,
Can fulfil thy law's demands,
Could my zeal no respite know,
Could my tears forever flow;
All for sin could not atone,
Thou must save and thou alone.

Nothing in my hand I bring,
Simply to thy cross I cling;
Naked come to thee for dress,
Helpless, look to thee for grace:
Foul I to the fountain fly,
Wash me, Saviour, or I die.

While I draw this fleeting breath,
When my eye-strings break in death,
When I soar to worlds unknown;
See thee on thy judgment throne,
Rock of ages cleft for me,
Let me hide myself in thee.

In the second stanza, every prop that sinful men
and women might be inclined to lean upon in making
themselves acceptable to God is swept away. Their attempts

to fulfill the righteous requirements of the law, their zeal, their tears—none of them suffice to save, for God alone can save sinners. The third stanza is a stark and simple expression of the real position that men and women find themselves in after all of their props are swept away. All of their doing and being before God is utterly inadequate to merit salvation—they desperately need his saving grace.

As witnessed then in Whitefield's preaching, Grimshaw's confession, and Toplady's hymn, justification by faith alone was every bit as central to the eighteenth-century Evangelical Revival as it was to the Reformation.

Union with Christ

From his own experience immediately before his conversion in 1735, Whitefield had learned that striving with all of one's might to do what was right and moral had been no solution for his guilt-ridden state. There needed to be a new birth, for he, like all of humanity, was dead in his sins, and there needed to be a brand-new beginning in which his sins were totally forgiven. Whitefield also emphasized that this experience of being born again and being justified by faith is not simply a bare outward profession of faith and divine legal declaration. Rather, as Whitefield insisted in his sermon entitled *On Regeneration*, believers are 'mystically united to him [i.e. Christ] by a true and lively faith, and thereby ... receive spiritual virtue from him, as the members of the natural body do from the head, or the branches from the vine.'

This theme of union with Christ, central to certain parts

of the theological tradition inherited by Whitefield—
notably it is a major theme in the writings of John
Calvin—is found throughout his preaching. In his sermon
on 1 Corinthians 1:30, Whitefield can thus exclaim: 'Oh,
what a privilege is this! To be changed from beasts into
saints, and from a devilish, to be made partakers of a divine
nature; to be translated from the kingdom of Satan, into
the kingdom of God's dear Son!' And in the same sermon,
Whitefield develops this theme at great length and with
rich biblical citations and allusions:

> [*Christians*] *are made partakers of a divine nature, and from
> Jesus Christ, they receive grace for grace; and every grace that
> is in Christ, is copied and transcribed into their souls; they are
> transformed into his likeness; he is formed within them; they
> dwell in him, and he in them; they are led by the Spirit, and
> bring forth the fruits thereof; they know that Christ is their
> Emmanuel, God with and in them; they are living temples of
> the Holy Ghost. And therefore, being a holy habitation unto the
> Lord, the whole Trinity dwells and walks in them; even here,
> they sit together with Christ in heavenly places, and are vitally
> united to him, their head, by a living faith; their Redeemer,
> their Maker, is their husband; they are flesh of his flesh, bone of
> his bone; they talk, they walk with him, as a man talketh and
> walketh with his friend; in short, they are one with Christ, even
> as Jesus Christ and the Father are one.*

Alongside the doctrines of the new birth and justification
by faith alone, union with Christ clearly lies at the heart
of Whitefield's thinking about the Christian life. It is the
ground for the new birth and justification, which we have

examined in this chapter, as well as the wellspring of gospel holiness that will occupy the discussion of the next. And it is an area of theological emphasis that modern-day Evangelicals need to recover.

6

Bearing witness to the work of the Holy Spirit

The new birth and justification by faith alone were hallmarks of Whitefield's spirituality, but so also was a concern for personal and social holiness. Whitefield never flagged in emphasizing that our acceptance with God can never be based on our sanctification, for the believer's sanctification is always incomplete in this life in a practical sense. Sin, to some degree, still indwells him. 'Our most holy thoughts', Whitefield wrote to a friend in early 1741, 'are tinctured with sin, and want the atonement of the Mediator'. But although faith alone saves, saving faith is never alone. It always issues in good works.

'Keep up a holy walk with God'
In the sermon *Christ, the Believer's Wisdom, Righteousness,*

Sanctification and Redemption Whitefield thus explicitly rejected the error of those practical Antinomians who 'talk of Christ without, but know nothing of a work of sanctification wrought within'. As Whitefield stressed, 'it is not going back to a covenant of works, to look into our hearts, and seeing that they are changed and renewed, from thence form a comfortable and well grounded assurance' of salvation. If 'we are not holy in heart and life, if we are not sanctified and renewed by the Spirit in our minds, we are self-deceivers, we are only formal hypocrites: for we must not put asunder what God has joined together'. In other words, believers cannot be in union with half a Christ. Or as he put it pithily in the sermon *The Lord our Righteousness*: 'if you are justified by the Blood, you are also sanctified by the Spirit of the Lord'.

Whitefield was also unsparing in his criticism of doctrinal Antinomianism, which on one occasion he succinctly defined as believers looking for 'all … Holiness without', that is, outside of themselves. In Whitefield's mind, the error of Antinomianism was so overemphasizing freedom from the condemnation of the law that the passionate pursuit of godliness in everyday life was downplayed. As he described it in a 1746 letter to Howel Harris: Antinomianism is a 'great Evil', 'a rank weed' sown by Satan. When doctrinal Antinomianism actually began to appear among Whitefield's English colleagues and supporters, in particular through the teaching of a man named William Cudworth, Whitefield fervently prayed in a letter to his mother Elizabeth Longden that Jesus might 'crush [this] Cockatrice in its bud'.

Following the lead of the New Testament Whitefield never implied that Christians must possess inherent holiness to be reckoned saints. However, he rightly assumed that those who have been made saints by faith alone will indeed lead holy lives. 'Live near to Christ', he wrote to an American correspondent, and 'keep up a holy walk with God. ... Hunger and thirst daily after the righteousness of Christ. Be content with no degree of sanctification'. Writing to his patroness, the Countess of Huntingdon, on the last day of 1755, he told her: 'Every day and every hour must we be passing from death to life. Mortification and vivification make up the whole of the divine work in the new-born soul'. Or as he put it to a friend in Philadelphia:

> I trust you will never rest till you are possessed of the whole mind which was in Christ Jesus. He is our pattern; and if we have true grace in our hearts, we shall be continually labouring to copy after our great exemplar. O the life of Jesus! How little of it is to be seen in those that call themselves his followers. Humility, meekness, love, peace, joy, goodness, faith, and the other blessed fruits of the Spirit, whither are they fled? I fear most take up with the shadow, instead of the substance. God forbid that I, or dear Mr. B—, should be of that unhappy number. Dear Sir, there is an unspeakable fulness, unsearchable riches in Christ. Out of him we are to receive grace for grace. Every grace that was in the Redeemer, is to be transcribed and copied into our hearts. This is Christianity; and without this, though we could dispute with the utmost clearness, and talk like angels, of the doctrines of grace, it would profit us nothing.

Whitefield wisely, and in New Testament fashion, sought
to keep the medium between two extremes. On the one
hand, he did not insist so much upon Christ's imputed
righteousness as to exclude the vital importance of the
believer having godliness to evidence that he or she belongs
to Christ. But nor did he give such priority to the believer's
inherent righteousness as to diminish his or her resting in
the righteousness of Jesus Christ alone for salvation.

JOHN WESLEY ON CHRISTIAN PERFECTION

Whitefield's perspective on the issue of holiness, though
it captures well New Testament thinking on the subject,
brought considerable grief to the evangelist. For he found
himself forced to defend it against two of his closest
friends, namely, John and Charles Wesley.

An honest evaluation of the eighteenth-century
Evangelical Revival cannot belittle the central role played
in it by the Wesley brothers. One thinks, for instance,
of John's fearless and indefatigable preaching of Christ
crucified for sinners year in and year out throughout the
length and breadth of Great Britain after his conversion
in 1738. Or there is the genius he displayed in preserving
the fruit of the revival in small fellowship groups called
'classes'. Again, one calls to mind the matchless hymnody of
Charles, whom J. I. Packer has rightly named 'the supreme
poet of love in a revival context'. Yet, for all the good that
John Wesley in particular did, he was a lightning-rod for
controversy. His propagation of evangelical Arminianism,
for example, did much to antagonize Whitefield and other
key evangelical leaders. On one occasion, for example,

Howel Harris told John Wesley: 'You grieve God's people by your opposition to electing love.'

Equally serious an error was John Wesley's commitment to the doctrine of Christian perfection. In the year before his death, he plainly indicated his conviction that God had raised up the Wesleyan Methodists primarily for the propagation of this doctrine. Yet, no other doctrine involved Wesley in more controversy than this one. It was a key factor in creating a rift between him and Whitefield, it alienated Wesley from many of the younger leaders in the revival, and eventually it even caused a slight division between him and his brother Charles.

Convinced that Scripture taught this doctrine, though, John Wesley was determined to publish it to the world. Yet, unlike his clear presentation of the heart of the gospel, his teaching about perfection is somewhat murky and at times difficult to pin down. He always contended that he was not advocating 'sinless perfection.' Yet, in his *A Plain Account of Christian Perfection* (1777), he could talk about the one who experienced this blessing as having 'sin ... separated from his soul' and having a 'full deliverance from sin'. Such perfection freed the person from evil thoughts and evil tempers. As he wrote to the Baptist authoress Ann Dutton in the summer of 1740, this blessing brings freedom from 'all faintness, coldness, and unevenness of love, both towards God and our neighbour. And hence from wanderings of heart in duty, and from every motion and affection that is contrary to the law of love'. All this sounds very much like sinless perfection despite Wesley's protest, 'we do not say that we have no sin *in us*, but that we do not *commit sin*.'

It is curious that Wesley himself never claimed to have experienced Christian perfection, or what he sometimes called 'the second blessing'. But as he preached it, others did, which to his mind was further confirmation of the scriptural truth of the doctrine. George Whitefield mentions in a letter that he wrote a friend in 1741 that he had met one of Wesley's followers who claimed he had not 'sinned in thought, word, or deed' for three months. This man affirmed that he was 'not only free from the power, but the very in-being of sin' and asserted that it was 'impossible for him to sin'. In the same letter Whitefield mentions another, a woman, who claimed she had been perfect for an entire year during which time she 'did not commit any sin'. When he asked her if she had any pride, she brazenly answered, 'No'! As Gordon Wakefield has wisely summed up Wesley's teaching on Christian perfection: it was 'confused, divisive, provoked scandals, errors, mania and the very evils of pride, malice and all uncharitableness it was intended to obliterate forever, and rested on an inadequate concept of sin'.

WHITEFIELD ON THE ERROR OF WESLEY'S TEACHING

It was from Whitefield that significant opposition to this teaching came first. Despite his friendship with John and almost deferential respect for him, Whitefield was not afraid to challenge his erroneous thinking on Christian discipleship. Between 1740 and 1742 he wrote letters to

Wesley and preached a number of sermons which opposed the latter's views about Christian perfection with frankness, but also with evident love. Writing on March 26, 1740, from Savannah, Georgia, for instance, he told Wesley that to the best of his knowledge 'no sin has dominion' over him, but he went on, 'I feel the strugglings of indwelling sin day by day'. Yet, despite his evident conflict with Wesley, he did not relish the prospect of disagreeing with him. Will not their disagreement, he said, 'in the end destroy brotherly love, and insensibly take from us that cordial union and sweetness of soul, which I pray God may always subsist between us?'

In September, 1740, Whitefield wrote to a Mr Accourt of London:

> *Sinless perfection ... is unattainable in this life. Shew me a man that could ever justly say, 'I am perfect'. It is enough if we can say so, when we bow down our heads and give up the ghost. Indwelling sin remains till death, even in the regenerate.*

Scriptural support for this position was found by Whitefield in texts like 1 Kings 8:46 ('there is no man that liveth and sinneth not') and James 3:2 ('In many things we all offend'), as well as examples drawn from the lives of King David and the Apostles Peter and Paul.

Two months later, Whitefield told Wesley: 'I am yet persuaded you greatly err. You have set a mark you will never arrive at, till you come to glory'. The following month found Whitefield wintering at Bethesda in Georgia. From there he published an open letter against Wesley in which he once again dealt plainly with his Christian brother. On the subject of perfection he confessed that since his conversion he has 'not doubted a quarter of an hour of having a saving interest in Jesus Christ'. But, he also had to acknowledge 'with grief and humble shame ... I have fallen into sin often'. Such a confession, though, was not unique to him: it was the 'universal experience and acknowledgment ... among the godly in every age'. Whitefield's perspective rests squarely on the testimony of Scripture, an adequate theological analysis of indwelling sin, and the testimony of God's people in the history of the church.

JOHN WESLEY'S LEGACY AND CHARLES WESLEY'S POSITION

Wesley's teaching carried enormous weight in the century after his death in 1791. It formed the heart and substance of the transatlantic holiness movement of the nineteenth century. And taking the nomenclature that John Fletcher, Wesley's godly lieutenant, used for Christian perfection, namely his description of it as 'the baptism of the Holy Spirit', Wesleyan perfectionism prepared the soil for the emergence of Pentecostalism in the twentieth century. What would the later history of Evangelicalism have been like if Wesley had listened to Whitefield? We have no way of knowing, of course, for God's sovereignty deemed otherwise. But it strikes this writer that his brother Charles eventually came to a much more balanced and clearer perspective on this matter than John, a perspective that was essentially the position of Whitefield. Writing to the great Yorkshire evangelist William Grimshaw in March of

1760, the younger Wesley stated: 'My perfection is to see my own imperfection; my comfort, to feel that I have the world, flesh, and devil to overthrow through the Spirit and merits of my dear Saviour; and my desire and hope is, to love God with all my heart, mind, soul, and strength, to the last gasp of my life. This is my perfection. I know no other, expecting to lay down my life and my sword together.'

THE QUESTION OF 'ENTHUSIASM'

This debate between Whitefield and Wesley over the nature of the Spirit's work in sanctification was not the only area of the doctrine of the Holy Spirit about which they disagreed. They approached the question of the various phenomena of the Evangelical Revival from differing vantage-points. In many areas touched by this revival, there occurred a variety of unusual physical and emotional manifestations, such as uncontrollable trembling and weeping, jumping, falling to the ground, striking dreams and visions. During the Scottish revival at Cambuslang near Glasgow in the summer of 1742, for instance, Whitefield was preached to huge, receptive audiences. In August, for instance, some 30,000 are said to have attended an outdoor communion service, where Whitefield preached a number of sermons over the course of a three-day weekend. Alexander Webster, a minister from Edinburgh, wrote of some of the happenings of that weekend:

During the time of divine worship, solemn, profound reverence overspread every countenance. They hear as for eternity ... Thousands are melted into tears. Many cry out in the bitterness of their soul. Some ... from the stoutest man to the tenderest child, shake and tremble and a few fall down as dead. Nor does this happen only when men of warm address alarm them with the terrors of the law, but when the most deliberate preacher speaks of redeeming love.

Similar phenomena happened in Wales the following year. Howel Harris, the Welsh evangelist who left an indelible mark on Welsh evangelicalism, informed Whitefield in March, 1743 of what God the Holy Spirit was doing through the preaching of his fellow evangelist and countryman, Daniel Rowland:

I was last Sunday at the ordinance [of the Lord's Supper] with Brother Rowland where I saw, felt and heard such things as I can't send on paper any idea of. The power that continues with him is uncommon. Such crying out and heart breaking groans, silent weeping and holy joy, and shouts of rejoicing I never saw ... 'Tis very common when he preaches for scores to fall down by the power of the Word, pierced and wounded or overcom'd by the love of God and sights of the beauty and excellency of Jesus, and lie on the ground ... Some lye there for hours. Some praising and admiring Jesus, free grace, distinguishing grace, others wanting words to utter.

To most of the intellectuals of that day, glorying as they did in reason, moderation and order, these scenes of the Revival in Scotland and Wales were sheer 'enthusiasm' or fanaticism. Now, to be charged with enthusiasm in the sphere of religion in the eighteenth century was to be accused of claiming extraordinary revelations and powers from the Holy Spirit, though the word could be used more loosely to denote any kind of religious excitement. The English philosopher John Locke, in his epoch-making work *An Essay concerning Human Understanding* (1689), used the word to denote the mindset of those who have 'an opinion of a greater familiarity with God, and a nearer admittance to his favour than is afforded to others', and have thus persuaded themselves that they have an 'immediate intercourse with the Deity, and frequent communications from the divine Spirit'. Clearly dependent upon Locke, the literary figure and pioneer of the English dictionary, Samuel Johnson, defined enthusiasm as 'a vain belief of private revelation; a vain confidence of divine favour or communication'. To all intents and purposes George Whitefield actually agreed with such a definition. 'The quintessence of enthusiasm', he declared in a sermon first published in 1746, was 'to pretend to be guided by the Spirit without the written word'. All inner impressions must be tried by 'the unerring rule of God's most holy word', and if found incompatible, rejected as 'diabolical and delusive'. From personal experience Whitefield knew of the dangerous shoals of enthusiasm, for he later realized that in the first few years of his ministry he had been occasionally imprudent in relying on subjective impressions.

However, if Whitefield and other leaders in the revival were wary of falling prey to enthusiasm, their critics were certain that they had succumbed. Two early criticisms can be taken as representative of the charges levelled against Whitefield and the revival in general. John Barker, an English Presbyterian minister, wrote to Philip Doddridge, a friend of Whitefield, on May 24, 1739, to tell him that he had heard Whitefield preaching in London in the open air and later also at Bath. Though he thought him sincere, Barker told Doddridge:

I still fancy that he is but a weak man,—much too positive, says rash things, and is bold and enthusiastic. I am most heartily glad to hear of piety, prayer, reformation, and every thing that looks like faith and holiness, in the North or South, the East or the West, and that any real good is done anywhere to the souls of men, but whether these Methodists are in a right way, whether they are warrantable in all their conduct, whether poor people should be urged (through different persons, successively) to pray from four in the morning till eleven at night, is not clear to me; and I am less satisfied with the high pretences they make to the Divine influence. I think what Mr. Whitfield says and does comes but little short of an assumption of inspiration or infallibility.

And as we have seen in a previous chapter, Joseph Butler, the Bishop of Bristol, also criticized Whitefield and his fellow evangelist John Wesley for what he perceived to be enthusiasm. In an interview with Wesley on August 18, 1739, Butler accused both of the evangelists of 'pretending to extraordinary revelations and gifts of the Holy Ghost', which he found 'a horrid thing—a very horrid thing'. Wesley denied this charge and stated that he sought only 'what every Christian may receive and ought to expect and pray for'.

WHITEFIELD AND WESLEY ON THE EXTRAORDINARY GIFTS OF THE SPIRIT

If he had been present Whitefield would also have strongly disputed the accuracy of Butler's accusation, for he was adamant that the extraordinary gifts of the Spirit, such as prophecy, speaking in tongues, and miraculous powers, had ceased with the passing of the apostles. In his sermon *The Indwelling of the Spirit, the Common Privilege of All Believers*, which John Wesley helped him edit for publication in the summer of 1739, Whitefield declared that Christ's promise of the Spirit in John 7:37–39 has nothing to do with receiving power 'to work miracles, or show outward signs and wonders'. Whitefield suggested that such signs and wonders occurred only when 'some new revelation was to be established, as at the first settling of the Mosaic or gospel dispensation' Indeed, he continued:

> *I cannot but suspect the spirit of those who insist upon a repetition of such miracles at this time. For the world being now become nominally Christian (though God knows, little of its power is left among us) there need not outward miracles, but only an inward co-operation of the Holy Spirit with the word, to prove that Jesus is the Messiah which was to come into the world.*

The only major group of individuals in the English-speaking Protestant world at that time who insisted upon the 'repetition' of the miracles which occurred in the early church were the French Prophets. This group had had its origins among the Protestants of southern France, who, had been savagely persecuted by the Roman Catholic

French state in the last half of the seventeenth century. In this crucible of persecution a movement had arisen, which was replete with visions, prophecies, speaking in tongues, and trances, and in which young people were especially prominent. In the summer of 1706, three prophets from this movement appeared in London. Within the space of a couple of years there were close to four hundred French Prophets, as they came to be called, and their charismatic manifestations had caused considerable public interest and consternation among the churches in the English capital. A turning-point for the movement, though, came in the summer of 1708 when it was prophesied that one of their number who had died, Thomas Emes, would be resurrected on May 25 from his grave in Bunhill Fields, the burying-ground for London Dissenters. When the predicted resurrection failed to transpire, the French Prophets became increasingly withdrawn and quiescent. With the beginning of the Evangelical Revival in the mid-1730s, however, the voices of the French Prophets once again were heard in Great Britain as they sought to win recruits for their own movement from among those involved in the revival.

Now, it is plain from the text cited above, that Whitefield would not have at all been impressed with the claims of the French Prophets to possess the extraordinary gifts of the Spirit. From his perspective, genuine manifestations of these gifts occurred only to authenticate the giving of fresh revelation. 'The world being now become nominally Christian'—that is, the 'world' having intellectually accepted the truth of Christianity—the Spirit's work was circumscribed to making this intellectual commitment a reality in heart and life. In arguing for such a cessationist position with regard to the gifts, Whitefield was simply affirming what had come to be a theological axiom for most eighteenth-century English-speaking Protestants. As Philip Doddridge plainly stated on one occasion:

> *It is of great importance ... to recollect ... that many things in Scripture, which relate to the operations of the Spirit of God on the mind, have a reference to those extraordinary gifts, which were peculiar to the apostles, and in which we of these later ages have no further concern, than as the general knowledge of them may establish our regard to the writings of those eminent servants of Christ, who were wisely and graciously distinguished by their divine Master, by such extraordinary endowments, to fit them for the extraordinary office they sustained.*

Whitefield would have wholeheartedly agreed with Doddridge. John Wesley would not have, though, for he was thoroughly convinced that the miraculous gifts of the Spirit definitely continued beyond the close of the New Testament era. Christian literature from the second and third centuries, Wesley maintained, contains clear evidence for the existence of these gifts. It was only when Constantine came to imperial power in the first quarter of the fourth century and began to favour the church that these gifts started to disappear. In a sermon on 1 Corinthians 12:31, which first appeared in the July and August 1787 issues of *The Arminian Magazine*, Wesley declared:

It does not appear that these extraordinary gifts of the Holy Ghost were common in the church for more than two or three centuries. We seldom hear of them after that fatal period when the Emperor Constantine called himself a Christian, and from a vain imagination of promoting the Christian cause thereby heaped riches, and power, and honour, upon the Christians in general; but in particular upon the Christian clergy. From this time they almost ceased; very few instances of the kind were found. The cause of this was not (as has been vulgarly supposed) 'because there was no more occasion for them' because all the world was become Christian. This is a miserable mistake: not a twentieth part of it was then nominally Christian. The real cause was: 'the love of many—almost of all Christians, so called—was 'waxed cold'. The Christians had no more of the Spirit of Christ than the other heathens. ... This was the real cause why the extraordinary gifts of the Holy Ghost were no longer to be found in the Christian church—because the Christians were turned heathens again, and had only a dead form left.

These reflections on the history of the gifts in the early church are not necessarily the best source for actually discovering what happened in these early centuries. Notwithstanding, this is an important text, for Wesley succinctly rejected the reason posited by Whitefield for the cessation of the gifts. In no uncertain terms he labelled it a 'miserable' misconception. Wesley granted that there did occur a cessation of the gifts, but he located it in the middle of the fourth century and not, as Whitefield and most other eighteenth-century English-speaking Protestants were wont to do, at the end of the first. Wesley found the reason for the cessation of these gifts in the words of Matthew 24:12: the love of the church 'waxed cold', that is, her love for God and the charismatic presence of his Spirit decreased in proportion as her material wealth and temporal influence increased. Moreover, Wesley tempered his assertion with regard to the cessation of the gifts with the adverb 'almost'. The Methodist leader was not prepared to dogmatically assert that genuine occurrences of the extraordinary gifts of the Spirit cannot be found in the history of the church after the fourth century. In fact, the reason which he gave for their disappearance leaves open, in principle, the possibility of their being found in any age of the church. Where God is loved and the charismatic presence of his Spirit relished as in the pre-Constantinian church, there the gifts might be found.

On the other hand, as early as 1739, Whitefield had come to a very different perspective, as we have already seen. Speaking about such physical phenomena as trembling and physically collapsing to the ground, Whitefield argued that it was

> tempting God to require such signs. That there is something of God in it I doubt not; but the devil, I believe, does interpose. I think it will encourage the French Prophets, take people from the written word, and make them depend on visions, convulsions, etc, more than on the promises and precepts of the Gospel.

Whitefield did not deny that some of these manifestations could issue from God. Yet, he was rightly convinced that such manifestations can easily become the focus of attention and interest rather than the Scriptures, the unalloyed revelation of God.

7

PROMOTING A
CALVINISTIC SPIRITUALITY

It is not infrequently asserted that Whitefield did not have a truly lucid understanding of Calvinism as a body of divinity. As we have seen, he was an evangelist extraordinaire, an itinerant preacher of the Word first and foremost. He certainly never had the time to write out his own systematic treatise on Calvinism. Yet, he was well grounded in the essentials of this theological perspective, as a close reading of both his letters and his sermons reveals. As John Lewis Gilmore has noted of both his sermons and letters, Whitefield was well able to 'give a restatement of the classic doctrines of the Reformation in the simplest, most salient language, indicating a digestion of the great doctrines, thoroughly integrated into his thought processes.'

AN HEIR TO THE REFORMERS AND PURITANS

Very early on in his ministry he identified himself as an heir of the theology of the Reformers and the Puritans. Theirs was a theology that revelled in what Iain Murray has called 'the great related chain of truths revealed in the New Testament—the Father's electing love, Christ's substitutionary death on behalf of those whom the Father had given him, and the Spirit's infallible work in bringing to salvation those for whom it was appointed'. Writing, for instance, from Philadelphia in 1739 during his first American tour, Whitefield declared:

> Oh the excellency of the doctrine of election, and of the saints final perseverance, to those who are truly sealed by the Spirit of promise! I am persuaded, till a man comes to believe and feel these important truths, he cannot come out of himself; but when convicted of these, and assured of the application of them to his own heart, he then walks by faith indeed, not in himself, but in the Son of God, who died and gave himself for him. Love, not fear, constrains him to obedience.

The same day he wrote to another correspondent that 'election, free grace, free justification without any regard to works foreseen' are 'the truths of God' that 'agree with the written word, and the experiences of the all the saints in all ages'. During his ministry he freely admitted that his theological convictions were 'Calvinistical principles', argued that 'the great doctrines of the Reformation' were what those involved in the Evangelical Revival chiefly sought to propagate, hoped that he would adhere to 'the doctrines of grace' as found in the Anglican *Thirty-nine*

Articles and the *Westminster Confession of Faith* all of his life, openly defended those whom he called 'the good old Puritans and free-grace Dissenters', and was convinced that 'useful puritanical books' were vital reading for theological students. Whitefield was convinced that if it had not been for the Puritans and those whom he calls 'their successors, the free-grace Dissenters', England would have become utterly destitute of vital Christianity and so 'void of any spiritual aid in spiritual distresses'.

Illustrative of his love of Puritan literature is the following passage, a recommendation of the works of the Puritan evangelist John Bunyan, written towards the end of his life.

Ministers never write or preach so well as under the cross: the Spirit of Christ and of glory then rests upon them. It was this, no doubt, that made the Puritans of the last century such burning and shining lights. When cast out ... and driven from their respective charges to preach in barns and fields, in the highways and hedges, they in an especial manner wrote and preached as men having authority. Though dead, by their writings, they yet speak; a peculiar unction attends them to this very hour; and for these thirty years past I have remarked, that the more true and vital religion hath revived, either at home or abroad, the more the good old Puritanical writings, or authors of a like stamp, who lived and died in the communion of the Church of England, have been called for.

The final sentence in this text is particularly noteworthy, for it draws an explicit link between the Puritans and the

Evangelical Revival of Whitefield's own day. Moreover, this recommendation is rooted, as Whitefield notes, in thirty years of appreciative reading of the works of the Puritans.

READING THE PURITANS

Like his Puritan predecessors Whitefield valued the written word. And despite the busyness of his life, he found time to read and digest not only Bunyan's writings, but also such Puritan works as *Human Nature in Its Four-fold State* by Thomas Boston—Whitefield told Ralph Erskine that Boston's book had 'under God been of much service to my soul'—Thomas Goodwin's commentary on various passages from Paul's letter to the Ephesians, *The Christian in Complete Armour* by William Gurnall, and some of the works of John Owen. He also read and warmly recommended other Puritan divines, men like John Flavel, John Howe, Solomon Stoddard, Thomas Halyburton, and was familiar with the life of Philip Henry. A regular companion from the very beginning of his ministry to its end was Matthew Henry's *Exposition of the Old and New Testament*, a work that 'draws on a century of Puritan theology, Bible study and homiletics'. Henry, he said, was his 'favourite commentator'.

David Crump, in a study of eleven of Whitefield's sermons, notes the way in which Puritanism, 'not only in its theology but also in its method of evangelism', shaped Whitefield's preaching. And he suggests that a reading of evangelistic literature by Puritan preachers like Joseph Alleine and Richard Baxter 'will quickly show the influences which had molded Whitefield's evangelistic method'. Martyn Lloyd-Jones thus puts it well when he succinctly states that Whitefield 'lived in the Puritans and their writings'.

THE DOCTRINES OF GRACE

There is little doubt that, in part, Whitefield learned his Calvinism from his reading of the Puritans. But his Calvinism also came to him through a close reading of the Word of God. As he once declared publicly, Calvinism is 'Scriptural truth'. It was Scripture, not the Reformer, that taught him his Calvinism: 'I embrace the Calvinistic scheme', he noted, 'not because Calvin, but Jesus Christ has taught it to me'. Thus, he expressed his confidence to his friend James Hervey that Hervey could read Paul's letters to the Romans and Galatians and find there plainly written the doctrines of justification by faith alone and the imputation of Christ's righteousness to the ungodly.

Moreover, the doctrines of grace ran true to his Christian experience. Whitefield knew from his own experience and that of countless others he counselled that unless God sovereignly intervenes in a person's life, that person will never willingly leave the thraldom of sin and its tawdry pleasures for the heart-ravishing joys of knowing God in Christ. Men and women have 'a free will to go to hell, but none to go to heaven, till God worketh in him to will and to do after his good pleasure'. Humanity's plight is a direct result of the fall of Adam and Eve. As Whitefield summed up what has happened to humanity in his sermon *The Polite and Fashionable Diversions of the Age, destructive to Soul and Body* (1740):

> *When God first made man, he made him pure and upright,*
> *placed him in the Garden of Eden, gave him the privilege*
> *of eating of all the trees in the Garden, save the tree or*
> *knowledge, of good and evil, which stood in the midst thereof;*
> *but man did not long continue in this happy state, but being*
> *left to his own free will, he fell, that is, he broke the command*
> *which God had given him, and so laid himself and his posterity*
> *open unto the divine justice, for as he was our representative,*
> *we stood and fell in him, and the corruption of this first man is*
> *imputed to all his race. When man had thus broken the divine*
> *commands, the wrath of God was ready to fall on him ...*

Whitefield was never reticent to preach about humanity's fallen estate and original sin, 'which renders us liable to God's wrath and damnation.'

Salvation from this horrific future comes from God alone. As Whitefield continued in the sermon just cited:

> *... justice was willing to strike the wretch into hell, when*
> *mercy interpos'd, and the Lord Jesus Christ promis'd to make*
> *Satisfaction to his offended Father. Now, nothing short of the*
> *blood of the Lord Jesus Christ could have redeem'd you from*
> *wrath, from hell, from destruction ...*

Given the seriousness with which Whitefield took the human plight, it is readily understandable why he emphasized the necessity of the new birth and justification by faith alone, which we examined in a previous chapter.

Once a person has committed their life to Christ, that

person, Whitefield was fond of emphasizing, is now safe in the hands of God. In the final sermon that Whitefield ever preached in London, he encouraged his hearers with a reflection on John 10 and the loving power of the Good Shepherd to protect his flock. 'He holds them in his hand, that is, he holds them by his power; none shall pluck them there. There is always something plucking at Christ's sheep ... but "None shall pluck them out of my hand," says Christ.' Whitefield went on to remark: 'My brethren, upon this text I can leave my cares, and all my friends, and all Christ's sheep, to the protection of Christ Jesus' never-failing love.' In his sermon on 1 Corinthians 1:30, he exclaimed, 'Was there no other text in the Book of God, this single one sufficiently proves the final perseverance of true believers; for never did God yet justify a man, whom he did not sanctify; nor sanctify one, whom he did not completely redeem and glorify.'

This promise of God to keep his people and enable them to persevere was tightly linked by Whitefield to holy living and godly endurance, which we looked at in the previous chapter. Thus, he preached: 'If we be not holy in heart and life, if we be not sanctified and renewed by the Spirit in our minds, we are self-deceivers.' Commenting on Whitefield's focus on the necessity of obedience following conversion, historian James Gordon has written: 'Whitefield's Calvinism never for a moment tolerated the Antinomian heresy. Again and again he called Christians to a life of unsparing discipleship, ethical obedience, and determined perseverance.' True faith ought to work itself out in loving actions done in obedience to the Word of God. Such works are to be pursued because the 'never-failing' love of Jesus promises that all true believers will persevere.

DEBATING CALVINISM WITH WESLEY

Moreover, for Whitefield, this promise rested secure on the sovereign electing love of God the Father. Whitefield's most famous discussion of election is to be found in his thirty-one page *A Letter to the Reverend Mr. John Wesley: in Answer to His Sermon, Entitled, Free-Grace*, finished in Georgia a week or so after his twenty-sixth birthday in 1740. The previous year Wesley had preached and then subsequently published a sermon entitled *Free Grace* in which, among other things, he attacked the Calvinistic doctrine of election. After much deliberation and heart-searching as to respond or not, Whitefield finally decided to write an open letter to Wesley in order to 'earnestly plead for the truths which are clearly revealed in the Word of God'.

In this response, Whitefield addressed five major points made by Wesley about election in *Free Grace*:

(1) That the doctrine of election makes preaching vain;

(2) That this doctrine discourages the pursuit of holiness;

(3) That it reduces Christian joy;

(4) That it is unfair for men to suffer simply because they are not elected; and

(5) That the doctrine of election makes revelation pointless.

At each turn of Wesley's argument, Whitefield graciously yet forcefully replied to Wesley's thinking; again and again Whitefield pointed his friend back to the Word of God. For example, in response to Wesley's argument that the teaching of election destroys the pursuit of holiness, Whitefield reminded him that the Apostle Paul does not seem to see it as a problem in Colossians 3:12 where he challenges 'the elect of God' to 'put on ... kindness, humility, meekness'. Whitefield also employed his own walk with God to argue for his position. 'As for my own part', he wrote, 'this doctrine is my daily support: I should utterly sink under a dread of my impending trials, was I not firmly persuaded that God has chosen me in Christ from before the foundation of the world, and that now being effectually called, he will suffer none to pluck me out of his almighty hand.'

For Whitefield, the biblical teaching about election was also extremely practical when it came to living the Christian life. For instance, he maintained, 'Without the belief of the doctrine of election, and the immutability of the free love of God, I cannot see how it is possible that any should have a comfortable assurance of eternal salvation.' Whitefield was also convinced that men who said that they did not believe in this doctrine were at bottom being intellectually dishonest. As he put it in his journal: 'Whatever men's reasoning may suggest, if the children of God fairly examine their own experiences—if they do God justice, they must acknowledge that they did not choose God, but that God chose them. And if he chose them at all, it must be from eternity, and that too without anything foreseen in them'.

Given Whitefield's passion for preaching the gospel to all and sundry, which we looked at in Chapter 4, the Anglican evangelist obviously saw no contradiction between this passion and his Calvinistic views about election. As he later told Wesley in a 1741 letter that he wrote from Aberdeen: 'Though I hold particular election, yet I offer Jesus freely to every individual soul'. In his *Free Grace* Wesley had stated his conviction that preaching is 'needless to them that are elected' and 'useless to them that are not elected'. Whitefield saw matters differently. As far as he was concerned there was no contradiction at all:

O dear Sir, what kind of reasoning—or rather sophistry—is this! Hath not God, who hath appointed salvation for a certain number, appointed also the preaching of the Word as a means to bring them to it? Does anyone hold election in any other sense? And if so, how is preaching needless to them that are elected, when the gospel is designated by God himself to be the power of God unto their eternal salvation? And since we know not who are elect and who reprobate, we are to preach promiscuously to all. For the Word may be useful, even to the non-elect, in restraining them from much wickedness and sin. However, it is enough to excite to the utmost diligence in preaching and hearing, when we consider that by these means, some, even as many as the Lord hath ordained to eternal life, shall certainly be quickened and enabled to believe. And who

that attends, especially with reverence and care, can tell but he
may be found of that happy number?

Whitefield's wedding together of the biblical doctrine
of election with the free preaching of the gospel, namely,
the means by which God has ordained to bring about
faith in the lives of the elect, is well summarized by James
Gordon when he concludes that Whitefield 'embodied an
evangelistic Calvinism in which the theological principle
of sovereign grace and the Evangelical imperative of gospel
proclamation merged in a creative fusion.'

Whitefield was also certain that only the sovereign work
of God through the Spirit of Christ can give the believer
spiritual victory over the effects of indwelling sin and the
attacks of the devil. As Whitefield pointed out in an early
letter from 1739:

The doctrines of our election, and free justification in Christ
Jesus, are daily more and more pressed upon my heart. They
fill my soul with a holy fire, and afford me great confidence in
God my Saviour. Surely I am safe, because put into his almighty
arms. Though I may fall, yet I shall not utterly be cast away.
The Spirit of the Lord Jesus will hold, and uphold me.

For Whitefield also, the truth of Calvinist doctrine
was found in the fact that it 'lays the soul lower at the
foot of Jesus' than any other perspective. Writing from
Philadelphia on his first visit to the city in 1739, Whitefield
observed that it was 'the doctrines of the Reformation' that
did the most to 'debase man and exalt the Lord Jesus. ... All

others leave freewill in man, and make him, in part at least, a Saviour to himself'.

When the Connecticut carpenter Nathan Cole heard Whitefield preach on what was for Cole an unforgettable day—October 23, 1740—he came under deep conviction of his sinfulness as he heard Whitefield outline the spiritual implications of some aspects of Calvinistic truth. 'My old foundation was broken up, and I saw that my righteousness would not save me', Cole later wrote. 'I was convinced', he continued, 'of the doctrine of election: and went right to quarrelling with God about it; because that all I could do would not save me; and he had decreed from eternity who should be saved and who not'. After two years of spiritual turmoil Cole experienced the new birth and could cry out Whitefield-like: 'I thought I could die a thousand deaths for Christ, I thought I could have been trodden under foot of man, be mocked or any thing for Christ—Glory be to God'. Little wonder then that we find Whitefield's correspondence peppered with such doxological exclamations as 'O free grace! Sovereign, electing, distinguishing love!' Reformed theology was utterly central not only to Whitefield's personal experience and his preaching, but also to his understanding of revival and biblical spirituality.

8

IMPACTING THE BAPTISTS

Despite his gracious catholicity, George Whitefield never forgot that he was an Anglican. He had been ordained as a deacon and priest within the Church of England in 1736 and 1739 respectively and he never ceased to love her theology as found in *The Thirty-Nine Articles* and her style of worship. As he said on one occasion about the Church of England: 'I am a friend to her Articles [*The Thirty-Nine Articles*], ... I am a friend to her liturgy'. If Whitefield never forget his Anglican colours and roots, nor did the Dissenters among whom he often preached. The Dissenters had been forced out of the state church in the previous century and had been brutally persecuted by Anglicans between 1660 and 1688, before the advent of religious toleration. One of these Dissenting communities, the Particular or Calvinistic Baptists, had flourished despite this persecution; but after the Act of Toleration was passed May 24, 1689, they, like other

Dissenters, began to slowly stagnate and even decline.
And when it came to self-definition, far too many of them
defined themselves over against Anglicanism and obviously
its ministers like Whitefield.

For example, the most significant English Baptist
theologian at the turn of the eighteenth century was
Benjamin Keach, who was a prolific author. He argued
against the Quakers, those seventeenth-century
counterparts of modern-day Pentecostals; he wrote
allegories, now long forgotten, that in his day rivalled
those of John Bunyan in popularity and sales; he was a
pioneer in the congregational singing of hymns in a day
when singing was limited to the Psalter; and he published
a number of lengthy collections of sermons, including *A
Golden Mine Opened* (1694) and *Gospel Mysteries Unveiled*
(1701), which remain invaluable treasures for the study of
seventeenth-century Baptist thought. In his statements
about the church he expressed many of the convictions that
prevailed in the Calvinistic Baptist community for much of
the first two thirds of the eighteenth century. In one of his
sermons, for instance, Keach unequivocally states vis-à-vis
Ezekiel 34:14 that this text implies that God's people

> *shall wander no more on the mountains of error and heresy;
> Christ leads them out of all idolatry and superstition, out of
> Babylon and all false worship; they shall no more be defiled ...
> by the pollution of false churches, or with harlot worship; the
> church of Rome is called the mother of harlots. Are there no
> false churches but the Romish church? Yea, there are, no doubt;
> she hath whorish daughters, though not such vile and beastly*

harlots as the mother is; all churches that sprang from her,
or all of the like nature, in respect of their constitution, and
that retain many of her superstitious names, garbs, rites, and
ceremonies, no doubt they are her daughters. Were the gospel
churches national, or did they receive into those churches
profane persons? No, no, they were a separate people, and a
congregational and a holy community, being not conformable to
this world; and into such a church Jesus Christ brings his sheep.
And from hence it followeth, that he carries his lost sheep when
he hath found them into his own fold, or into some true gospel
church.

The Church of Rome is here denominated as the mother
of false worship. And though Keach does not explicitly
mention the Church of England by name, surely he has
in mind this body of churches when he talks about this
community being a 'whorish daughter' who has 'many
of her [i.e. Rome's] superstitious names, garbs, rites, and
ceremonies.'

Similarly, the leading Baptist theologian during the mid-
eighteenth century, John Gill of London, can state with
no equivocation: 'The Church of England has neither the
form nor matter of a true church, nor is the Word of God
purely preached in it'. A resolution passed by St. Mary's
Baptist Church, Norwich, in 1754 reveals the same attitude.
In the minute book for that year we read that 'it is unlawful
for any ... to attend the meetings of the Methodists, or to
join in any worship which is contrary to the doctrines and
ordinances of our Lord Jesus'. And in London, a weaver
and his wife by the name of Cricket were disfellowshipped

by a Baptist church for going to regularly hear Whitefield preach.

Not surprisingly many Calvinistic Baptists had deep reservations about the Revival since it was uniformly led by Anglicans. A few of these Anglican preachers were Arminian in theology, like the Wesley brothers, and thus definitely beyond the pale for the *Calvinistic* Baptists. However, Whitefield was a Calvinist. Yet, he was still an Anglican. In addition, the fervency of his evangelism and his passionate urging of the lost to embrace Christ prompted a number of Baptist critics—whose heightened Calvinism caused them to question the wisdom of Whitefield's evangelistic strategies—to complain of what they termed his 'Arminian accent'!

A good number of eighteenth-century Calvinistic Baptists were thus adamant in their refusal to regard the Evangelical Revival as a genuine work of God. From their perspective, it simply did not issue in 'true gospel churches'. These Baptists seem to have assumed that a revival could only be considered genuine if it preserved and promoted the proper form of the local church. For many Calvinistic Baptists of the first six or seven decades of the eighteenth century, outward form and inward revival went hand in hand. Their chief preoccupation was the preservation of what they considered the proper New Testament form of church. In their minds, when God brought revival it would have to issue in true gospel churches like theirs.

The dilemma facing these Baptists was not an easy

one. They rightly felt constrained to emphasize the New Testament idea of the local church as a congregation of visible saints and assert that the concept of a state church is antithetical to the whole tenor of the new covenant. Moreover, these were truths for which their forebears in the previous century had suffered much. To abandon them would have been unthinkable. But what then was to be made of the ministry of men like Whitefield?

One possible solution would have been for the eighteenth-century Calvinistic Baptists to have viewed the ministry of Whitefield and other Anglican Calvinists in the way that their seventeenth-century forebears viewed the labours of the sixteenth-century Reformers. The latter did not reject the ministry of the Reformers because they were not Baptists. Rather, they recognized that the Reformers had been greatly used by God to bring the church out of the theological ignorance of the late Middle Ages. Yet, though the Reformers did well, they failed to apply all that the Scriptures taught. As Benjamin Keach said with regard to the Particular Baptist community's recovery of key New Testament principles in the wake of the Reformation: 'Must we content ourselves with the light which the Church had in respect of this and other gospel-truths at the beginning of the Reformation,—since God hath brought forth greater (to the praise of his own rich grace) in our days?' Similarly, it could have been recognized that God was indeed at work in Whitefield's remarkable ministry and that of the other leaders of the Revival, but that there were certain areas—in particular, those dealing with the church and its nature—where they needed greater light.

WHITEFIELD AND THE ENGLISH BAPTISTS

Thankfully, there were some noteworthy exceptions, men and women who were prepared to risk a certain degree of ostracism from their own Baptist community to fellowship with Whitefield. In the Baptist cause in Leominster, for instance, there was John Oulton, who appears to have gotten to know Whitefield in April 1742 when he invited the Anglican evangelist to preach to his Baptist congregation. Although Whitefield was unable to accept this particular invitation, a friendship was formed and in 1743 Whitefield was able to preach twice at Oulton's request.

In London, Andrew Gifford had an extremely fruitful ministry as pastor of Eagle Street Baptist Church from 1735 till his death. A number of years prior to his death in 1780 some six hundred people had been converted under his preaching and eleven men sent into the pastorate from the congregation. He was an enthusiastic supporter of Whitefield's ministry and preached for him at Whitefield's Tottenham Court Road Tabernacle. Gifford's love of Whitefield's preaching led him to revise *Eighteen Sermons Preached by the late Rev. George Whitefield* for publication in 1771, the year after Whitefield's death. The volume was dedicated to Selina Hastings and Gifford expressed the hope that the sermons would continue to instruct despite the death of the one who had preached them, even as the sun, 'the glorious luminary of the heavens, ... seems visible, even after it is set, by the refraction of its resplendent rays'.

There was also an immense number of converts to

the Particular Baptist churches from the 1740s onwards, who received their first real understanding of the gospel through the voice of Whitefield. For example, William Nash Clarke, pastor of Unicorn Yard Baptist Church in London in the 1770s and early 1780s, had been converted under Whitefield's ministry when he was but ten years of age. Mary Andrews, a prominent member of Olney Baptist Church, owed her first lasting convictions of the Christian Faith to a sermon she heard Whitefield preach when she was but three or four years of age. The conversion of Samuel Medley, pastor of Byrom Street Baptist Church in Liverpool, in 1760 was owing both to the ministry of Whitefield and Andrew Gifford. John Fawcett, Sr. was fifteen when he first heard Whitefield preach in Yorkshire on John 3:14 in 1755. Fawcett had gone to church regularly, but he had never heard preaching like this before. By this one sermon alone he was given a clear view of 'God reconciled' to sinners 'through the atonement of a suffering Saviour'. Fawcett's 'unbelieving fears' were dispelled and he was filled with 'joy unspeakable, and full of glory'. For the rest of his life Fawcett kept a portrait of Whitefield in his study and the very mention of his name would prompt 'grateful remembrance'.

John Ryland, Sr., often wrongly accused of being a hyper-Calvinist because of remarks he made to a young William Carey, first heard Whitefield preach in Bristol when he was a student at the Baptist Academy there in the 1740s. Many years later, in 1767, when Ryland was pastoring in Northampton, he met with Whitefield for fellowship during one of the latter's last preaching tours in England.

And the following year, he took his son, John Ryland, Jr.,
later a close friend of Carey, to hear Whitefield preach one
of his final sermons in London. It appears that Ryland had
cultivated a friendship with Whitefield over the intervening
years.

WHITEFIELD'S FRIENDSHIP WITH ANNE DUTTON

Most amazingly, George Whitefield also found a spiritual
friend in a Baptist woman by the name of Anne Dutton.
Anne had been born in the early 1690s and become a
Particular Baptist around 1713. She was married to a
fellow Baptist named Thomas Cattell in 1715, who died
quite suddenly four years later. She subsequently married
Benjamin Dutton, probably in the summer of 1720. Her
husband accepted a call to the pastorate of the Baptist
cause in Great Gransden, Huntingdonshire, in the summer
of 1731, where he laboured till a trip to America in the mid-
1740s. This journey to America involved both preaching
and the promotion of his wife's books, but on the return
voyage in 1747 he was tragically drowned when the ship
sank in the Atlantic. By the time of Benjamin's death, Anne
was well on her way to becoming a well-known author
on both sides of the Atlantic. She had been writing for a
number of years before her husband's demise. After his
death a steady stream of tracts and treatises, collections
of selected correspondence, and poems poured forth from
her pen, making her, in the judgment of Michael D. Sciretti,
who has written a doctoral thesis on Dutton, 'probably
the most prolific woman writer in the eighteenth century,
Baptist or otherwise.'

Among her numerous correspondents were George Whitefield as well as Howel Harris, Selina Hastings, John Wesley, and William Seward. Sciretti has noted that in her letters to preachers like Harris and Whitefield she would attempt to inspire them 'by infusing them with confidence, intention, steadfastness, and courage, boldly urging them to greater service and devotion to Christ and the gospel.' William Seward, Whitefield's co-worker and confidant, had begun writing to Dutton early in 1739, for instance. When he read a letter she wrote to him in May, 1739, for instance, he found it 'full of such comforts and direct answers to what I had been writing that it filled my eyes with tears of joy.'

The correspondence that we have from Whitefield to Dutton and vice versa span the early years of Whitefield's ministry, from 1739 to 1744. But this was a critical period as well, for it was in this period that Whitefield was forming his doctrinal convictions about Calvinism. Dutton first heard of Whitefield in 1739 and was filled with joy at 'such a great work [being] done in the world by him.' By the time that the second extant letter that we have from Whitefield to Dutton came to be written in February 1741, the evangelist clearly considered Dutton a close friend. As he wrote to her: 'Help me by your prayers. It is an ease thus to unbosom one's self to a friend, and an instance of my confidence in you.' A few months later, Whitefield visited Dutton and said after their meeting, 'her conversation is as weighty as her letters.' Whitefield encouraged her to write to a number of his friends in South Carolina, including a Baptist pastor by the name of Isaac Chanler, the pastor of

Ashley River Baptist Church. 'You will excuse this freedom,' remarked Whitefield about this encouragement to Dutton to undertake a transatlantic correspondence, 'I am willing your usefulness should be as extensive as may be. May the Lord bless you ever, more and more.'

In one of her letters to Whitefield, she reminded the evangelist why his position in the debate with the Wesleys over Christian perfection was biblical. In little more than twelve hundred words, she provides a tightly and biblically reasoned argument as to why sinless perfection was not at all correct. Here we see why Whitefield considered Dutton's letters to be weighty and how Dutton helped the great evangelist to think through this issue biblically and stand firm in his convictions. From 1 John 3:2, for example, she maintained that

> our imperfection in holiness, which arises from the being and working of sin in our corrupt nature, is necessarily implied, ... [for] the Apostle says, 'When he shall appear, we shall be like him; for we shall see him as he is'. He doth not say we are like him; ... but we shall be like him. And [he] gives the great cause of this great effect: for we shall see him as he is. Sight of Christ is the cause of likeness to him. Sight of Christ partial in this life produceth partial likeness. Sight of Christ total in the life to come will produce total likeness to him. First in our souls, during a separate state, and then in our whole persons after the resurrection of the just. Then, and not till then, shall we be perfectly like Christ, in holiness and glory. Holiness, which is the glory of the soul, is the effect of us beholding the glory of the Lord, as 2 Corinthians 3:18. But we all with open face,

beholding 'as in a glass the glory of the Lord, are changed in the same image, from glory to glory, as by the Spirit of the Lord'. Whence we may likewise note, that the change of the soul into the image of God, is imperfect, with respect to degrees, and a progressive work while in this life: it is from glory to glory. The New Testament saints, if compared with the Old, have an open-faced view of the glory of God in Christ; and a more glorious change into his image. But if compared with that vision of God which we shall have in glory, we see but darkly.

WHITEFIELD AND THE AMERICAN BAPTISTS

As we have seen, George Whitefield crossed the Atlantic thirteen times and preached in virtually every major town on the Atlantic seaboard and numerous American Baptists came to openly support the ministry of the English preacher. In the South Carolina low country, Isaac Chanler invited Whitefield to address overflowing crowds at his church in July of 1740. And in a sermon that Chanler delivered that same year, he prayed for Whitefield by name: 'May blessed Whitefield long live an extensive blessing to the Church of God!' Oliver Hart was not slow to speak about the enormous benefits that he had derived from listening to Whitefield's sermons, both in his native Pennsylvania and in South Carolina where he pastored First Baptist Church in Charleston from 1750 to 1780. And when Euhaw Baptist Church began worshipping in a new meeting-house in March, 1752, Whitefield was asked to give the first sermon in the building.

In Pennsylvania, during Whitefield's first trip to America in 1739, Whitefield developed a friendship with Jenkin

Jones, a Welsh Baptist who was pastoring First Baptist Church in Philadelphia at the time and whom Whitefield considered to be 'a spiritual man'. Whitefield was deeply impressed with some of the members of his church, who, he noted in his diary, 'loved the Lord Jesus in sincerity'. When Whitefield heard Jones preach the following year, he commented that he was the only minister in Philadelphia 'who speaks feelingly and with authority'.

One of those converted under Whitefield's preaching during this trip was an African-American woman, who later began to worship with Jenkin Jones in the Philadelphia Baptist meeting-house. On one occasion when Jones was away and another Welsh Baptist was preaching, 'the Word came with such power to her heart', Whitefield recorded in his diary, 'that at last she was obliged to cry out; and a great concern fell upon many in the congregation'. Some of those in the meeting-house, thinking her mad and 'full of new wine', told her to be quiet, but she continued to shout out loud expressions of praise. When Whitefield talked to her, what she told him seemed 'rational and solid, and I believe in that hour the Lord Jesus took a great possession of her soul'. In fact, Whitefield was sure that when God called a significant number of African-Americans to faith in Christ, 'God will highly favour them, ... wipe off their reproach, and show that he is no respecter of persons, but that whosoever believeth in him shall be saved'.

Not all American Baptists, however, looked on the impact of Whitefield's ministry favourably. Ebenezer

Kinnersley, a highly respected scientist and tutor at the College of Philadelphia, as well as friend of Benjamin Franklin, was also a Baptist lay preacher and an assistant pastor with Jenkin Jones. According to an account in the *Philadelphia Gazette* of a July 1740 sermon Kinnersley preached at Philadelphia's First Baptist, he was unsparing in his denunciation of Whitefield and those who imitated his affective style of preaching:

> What spirit such enthusiastic ravings proceed from, I shall not attempt to determine, but this I am sure of, that they proceed not from the Spirit of God; for our God is a God of order, and not of such confusion ... such whining, roaring harangues, big with affected nonsense, have no other tendency, but to operate on the softer passions, and work them up to a warm pitch of enthusiasm.

In New England, reaction among Baptists to Whitefield's itinerant ministry was also divided. For example, the refusal of Jeremiah Condy, pastor of the First Baptist Church of Boston, to support Whitefield led to a schism in his church in 1742 and the eventual formation of the Second Baptist Church. Whitefield's ministry also became the impetus for the emergence of an entire generation of important Baptist leaders, men like Isaac Backus and Shubal Stearns.

THE CONVERSION OF ROBERT ROBINSON

The story of one Baptist converted under Whitefield's preaching warrants more extensive notice. When Robert Robinson first went to hear Whitefield preach his motivation in going was an odd one to say the least. On Sunday morning, May 24, 1752, he and some friends were out looking for some amusement when they came across an aged woman who claimed to be a fortune-teller. After they had gotten her thoroughly drunk on what was probably cheap gin, they proceeded to have her tell their fortunes. When it came to Robinson, the woman predicted that he would live to see his children, grandchildren, and even great-grandchildren growing up around him.

Now, what had started as something of a lark was taken quite seriously by Robinson as he made his way home later that day. When he was alone, he thought that if he were indeed to live to such a ripe age, he would probably end up being a burden to his family. There were in those days no such things as social security or welfare. What then could he do? Well, he thought, one way for those who are older to make themselves liked by their grandchildren is to have a good stock of stories to draw upon to entertain them. He thus determined there and then to fill his mind with knowledge and 'everything that is rare and wonderful', which, when he was old, would stand him in good stead and cause him, so he reasoned, to 'be respected rather than neglected'.

As his first acquisition, he decided to experience one of Whitefield's sermons. He went to hear him, though, as he later told the famous preacher, with feelings of pity for 'the folly of the preacher' and 'the infatuation of the hearers'—those 'poor deluded Methodists',—and of abhorrence for Whitefield's doctrine. Whitefield was preaching that evening at the Tabernacle, his meeting-house in Moorfields, London. His text was Matthew 3:7, John the Baptist's stern rebuke of the Pharisees and the Sadducees, 'O generation of vipers, who hath warned you to flee from the wrath to come?' When, according to Robinson,

Mr. Whitefield described the Sadducean character; this did not touch me, I thought myself as good a Christian as any man in England. From this he went to that of the Pharisees. He described their exterior decency, but observed that the poison of the viper rankled in their hearts. This rather shook me. At length, in the course of his sermon, he abruptly broke off; paused for a few moments; then burst into a flood of tears; lifted up his hands and eyes, and exclaimed, 'O my hearers! the wrath's to come, the wrath's to come!' *These words sunk into my heart, like lead in the waters. I wept, and when the sermon was ended, retired alone. For days and weeks I could think of little else. Those awful words would follow me, wherever I went,* 'The wrath's to come, the wrath's to come'!

For over three years Robinson was haunted by these words and Whitefield's sermon. He regularly attended the preaching at the Tabernacle, and found himself 'cut down for sin' and 'groaning for deliverance'. Eventually on Tuesday, December 10, 1755, 'after having tasted the pains of rebirth', Robinson 'found full and free forgiveness through the precious blood of Jesus Christ'. About two and a half years after his profession of faith Robinson wrote a hymn long treasured by God's people: 'Come thou

Fount of every blessing'. It appears to have been written to commemorate what God did for him when he saved him.

> Come thou Fount of every blessing!
> Tune our hearts to sing Thy grace!
> Streams of mercy never ceasing,
> Call for songs of loudest praise!
> Teach us some melodious sonnet,
> Sung by flaming tongues above;
> Praise the mount—Oh fix us on it,
> Mount of God's unchanging love!

Whitefield later included this hymn in the hymnal he designed for use at the Tabernacle in London, *A Collection of Hymns for Social Worship*.

After a short career as a Methodist preacher, Robinson went on to build a thriving work at St. Andrew's Street Baptist Church, Cambridge, where he became known as one of the finest preachers in England. Sadly, though, there is evidence of doctrinal confusion in the final decade of his life, the 1780s.

CODA

Olin C. Robison, in a fine study of the English Particular Baptist community between 1760 and 1820, has stated that 'more than any other individual, George Whitefield was responsible for the awakening of Dissent to a spirit of revival in the eighteenth century'. There is little doubt that this is true of that wing of English Dissent known as the Particular Baptists. And in America, Whitefield was a major influence in the emergence of the Baptists as a major force in American Christianity.

9

WHITEFIELD THE CELEBRITY

I n his day, there is little doubt that Whitefield was a celebrity, even something of an icon. Whitefield's foes deemed this to be evidence that he was an 'enthusiast' and guilty of self-promotion. Even friends like Philip Doddridge could query, 'who can wonder if so much popularity has a little intoxicated him?' But, reading his correspondence especially, it appears that it was ever Whitefield's desire that he please his God and Saviour first and foremost. His passion seems to have been that God and Jesus Christ, the ones about whom the Word chiefly spoke, were to be glorified and not he himself, the preacher of the Word.

A distinct Christ-centredness permeates his correspondence. 'What unsearchable riches are there in Jesus [Christ], he told Jonathan Thompson in the summer of 1746. 'What treasures of light & love are hid in Him! May this find you gazing at & admiring them, & by a living faith drawing them down into your soul'. Writing around the same time to John Redman, an American who was studying at Guy's Hospital in London and who later became a renowned physician in Philadelphia, he expresses a similar desire. He hoped that his letter found Redman

admiring the love & beauty of the Great and everblessed Physician of souls. Blessed be God that I hear you have His interest yet at heart. Look up to Him, my Dear Man, & you shall be kept unspotted from the world. London is a dangerous place. But Jesus is able to deliver you, & make you more than Conqueror over all temptations. May He carry you as a Witness of the power of his resurrection by Land & by sea, & after death give you a Eternal & exceeding weight of glory!

The following year he was moved to exclaim in a letter he wrote while in New York:

Christ is a good Master: he is worthy of all our time, and of everything that we possess. Is not one heart too little for him? And yet he requires no more. Amazing love! I am lost when I think of it. I can only say, Lord, I adore and worship!

His ideal in this regard is found in some lines he wrote in May of 1746 to William Pepperell, the commander of the New England militia that had captured the fortress of Louisbourg the previous year: 'Glory be to our God for what He had done for you & by you, & above all, for enabling you like a pure crystal to transmit all the honour he has been pleased to pour upon you, back again to the source from whence it first sprang'. Three years later he applied the image of the light-transmitting crystal to himself: 'Like a pure crystal, I would transmit all the glory he is pleased to pour upon me, and never claim as my own, what is his sole property.'

In his correspondence, though, Whitefield frequently admitted to wrestling with pride and indwelling sin. 'It is difficult', he observed early on in his ministry, 'to go through the fiery trial of popularity and applause untainted'. This observation came from bitter experience. 'I am a proud, imperious, sinful worm', he wrote to Gabriel Harris in 1737. Four years later, we find the same self-evaluation: 'I am a poor unworthy sinner, and yet, (O sovereign grace!) the Lord works by me day by day'. And in 1755 he cried out in a letter to Selina Hastings:

O this self-love, this self-will! It is the devil of devils. Lord Jesus, may thy blessed Spirit purge it out of all our hearts! But O how must the divine Paraclete sit as a refiner's fire upon the heart, in order to bring this about! Few choose such fiery purgations, and therefore so few make the progress that might justly be expected of them in the divine life. Make me, O God, willing to be made, willing to be, to do, or suffer what thou pleasest, and then—what then?—this foolish fluttering heart will sweetly be moulded into the divine image.

In the year this text was written Protestant Britain was on the brink of war with Catholic France—a war that would last until 1763 and would become known as the Seven Years' War—and there was widespread fear of Roman Catholic domination if this war should be lost. Whitefield's main concerns, however, were elsewhere. He could pray for a British victory, but he was convinced that the believer's chief danger and fiercest warfare was with indwelling sin. 'O that this time of outward danger', he wrote towards the end of autumn, 1755, 'may be sanctified to the exciting of greater zeal against our inward spiritual enemies! For after all, the man of sin in our own hearts, is the greatest foe the real Christian hath to fear'.

Nor did this sense of his own sinfulness keep Whitefield silent. In fact, it had the opposite effect. As he told a friend in 1742:

> It is good to see ourselves poor, and exceeding vile; but if that sight and feeling prevent our looking up to, and exerting ourselves for our dear Saviour, it becomes criminal, and robs the soul of much comfort. I can speak this by dear-bought experience. How often have I been kept from speaking and acting for God, by a sight of my own unworthiness; but now I see that the more unworthy I am, the more fit to work for Jesus, because he will get much glory in working by such mean instruments; and the more he has for given me, the more I ought to love and serve him. Fired with a sense of his unspeakable loving-kindness, I dare to go out and tell poor sinners that a lamb was slain for them; and that he will have mercy on sinners as such, of whom indeed I am chief.

Thus, despite the intensity of this inner struggle, Whitefield could sincerely declare: 'Let my name be forgotten, let me be trodden under the feet of all men, if Jesus may thereby be glorified'.

FURTHER READING

For Whitefield's own words, see *George Whitefield's Journals* (London: The Banner of Truth Trust, 1960); *George Whitefield's Letters* (Carlisle, PA: The Banner of Truth Trust, 1976); *The Sermons of George Whitefield*, ed. Lee Gatiss (Wheaton, IL: Crossway, 2012), 2 vols; *The Works of George Whitefield on CD-ROM* (Weston Rhyn, England: Quinta Press, 2000); links to additional material can be found at http://www.quintapress.com/whitefield. htm (accessed August 6, 2014).

The best biographical studies of Whitefield are those of Arnold A. Dallimore, *George Whitefield: The Life and Times of the Great Evangelist of the Eighteenth-Century Revival* (1970 and 1979 eds.; reprinted Westchester, Illinois: Cornerstone Books, 1979 and 1980), 2 vols., and Thomas S. Kidd, *George Whitefield: America's Spiritual Founding Father* (New Haven, CT: Yale University Press, 2014). Dallimore has also written a one-volume account of Whitefield's life, which has been recently re-issued: *George Whitefield: God's Anointed Servant in the Great Revival of the Eighteenth Century* (1990 ed.; reprinted Wheaton, IL: Crossway, 2010).

For two studies that are more critical and controversial in nature, see Harry S. Stout, *The Divine Dramatist: George Whitefield and the Rise of Modern Evangelicalism* (Grand Rapids, MI: William B. Eerdmans Publ. Co., 1991) and Frank Lambert, *'Pedlar in Divinity': George Whitefield and the Transatlantic Revivals, 1737–1770* (Princeton, NJ: Princeton University Press, 1994). For an insightful critique of Stout, see Eric Carlsson, 'Book Reviews: Harry S. Stout, *The Divine Dramatist: George Whitefield and the Rise of Modern Evangelicalism*', *Trinity Journal*, NS, 14, no. 2 (Fall 1993), 238–247.

For the unwitting role that Whitefield played in the founding of the United States, see the fine work by Jerome Dean Mahaffey, *Preaching Politics: The Religious Rhetoric of George Whitefield and the Founding of a New Nation* (Waco, TX: Baylor University Press, 2007) and his more recent *The Accidental Revolutionary: George Whitefield and the Creation of America* (Waco, TX: Baylor University Press, 2011).